InfoWorld: A DOS User's Guide to UNIX

Douglas Topham

BRADY

New York   London   Toronto   Sydney   Singapore   Tokyo

BRADY

Simon & Schuster, Inc.
15 Columbus Circle
New York, NY 10023

DISTRIBUTED BY PRENTICE HALL TRADE

Manufactured in the United States of America
10 9 8 7 6 5 4 3 2 1

Library of Congress Cataloging-in-Publication Data

Topham, Douglas W., 1942–
    A DOS User's guide to UNIX/Douglas Topham.
        p.   cm.
        1.UNIX (Computer operating system) I. Title.
QA76.76.063T66   1990
005.4'3—dc20   89-70869
                                                                              CIP

ISBN 0-13-219098-2

Acknowledgment

I would like to thank Bruce Webster, the reviewer of this book.

Limits of Liability and Disclaimer of Warranty

The author and publisher of this book have used their best efforts in preparing this book and the programs contained in it. These efforts include the development, research, and testing of the theories and programs to determine their effectiveness. The author and publisher shall not be liable in any event for incidental or consequential damages in connection with, or arising out of, the furnishing, performance, or use of these programs.

Registered Trademarks

CONTENTS

FOREWORD

Following our 1987 readership survey, (an astounding 20% requesting coverage of UNIX/XENIX) *InfoWorld* introduced its first UNIX special edition in March 1988—and a month later, instituted a UNIX section on a regular weekly basis.

The emergence of UNIX has (and will continue) to cast its shadow into every computational facet of the Fortune 1000: Now users can have the best of both worlds—the economical and computational independence of the MS-DOS PC, and the cohesion of a single departmental or company-wide UNIX database. Applications that are meant for teams of workers—which DOS environments are only now discovering as "groupware"—have long been staples of the UNIX application's environment.

These and other events have probably led you to this book. Douglas Topham provides you with an outstanding picture of the UNIX environment, taking you through a step-by-step introduction, complete with examples and illustrations. Designed from a DOS user's perspective, Doug clearly shows the direct correlations between DOS and UNIX. (In fact, many DOS features were derived from UNIX, so the similarities are striking.) I learned a lot about UNIX by reading this book, and in the process, also learned several things that I didn't know about DOS. And suprisingly enough, one doesn't have to "give up" the DOS world to get to the other side. You'll find you can productively operate from both ends of the bridge.

—J. Michael Lowe, Editor-in-Chief

CHAPTER 1

COMPARING DOS AND UNIX

Background

In 1980, IBM began to develop the original Personal Computer. At that time, the standard operating system for small systems was CP/M (control program/ monitor) from Digital Research. IBM called its operating system for the new machine PC-DOS, but it was nearly identical to CP/M. PC-DOS included nearly all the same commands, along with a number of improvements. For example, COPY replaced PIP, and a single DIR command replaced CP/M's DIR and STAT. PC-DOS was developed specifically for the IBM PC, but a closely related operating system known as MS-DOS was later designed for machines that were IBM-compatible.

At the time IBM PC was released, the UNIX operating system was over ten years old. The current release of UNIX was Version 7, but UNIX was changing rapidly. XENIX had just been released in 1980, AT&T was just about to release System III, and the University of California was just about to release 4.2BSD. UNIX was known mainly in universities and research institutions, but was beginning to be used in the engineering community.

Throughout the 1980s, while UNIX was making modest inroads into the commercial market, DOS skyrocketed to its preeminent position as a universal standard for small systems. In the meantime, DOS was borrowing more and more features from UNIX, partially erasing the differences between the two operating systems. DOS has much more in common with UNIX today than it did when the PC first appeared.

Common Features

Entering Commands

One thing DOS and UNIX have in common is the way you make the system work. With either system, you see a prompt on the screen when the system is ready to do something. In the blank space after the prompt, you enter a *command line* for the system to read. The command line consists of a command, followed by any number of *arguments* (possibly none). A command processor takes the command line, interprets its meaning, and causes the system to carry out the task that you have requested.

For example, suppose you want to make a copy of a file. Here is what would happen in each system, with DOS on the left and UNIX on the right:

DOS	UNIX

1. The system presents a prompt, indicating that it is ready to accept input from you:

```
C:\> _                              $ _
```

2. You type a command line and press the ENTER key:

```
C:\> COPY OLD NEW          $ cp old new
```

3. The system carries out the task you requested and displays another prompt on the screen:

```
C:\> COPY OLD NEW          $ cp old new
C:\> _                     $ _
```

Steps 1–3 show what happens when you enter a command line correctly and the system processes it successfully. If you make a mistake and the system cannot carry out the task, then steps 1–3 will look something like:

DOS	UNIX

1. The system presents a prompt, indicating that it is ready to accept input from you:

```
C:\> _                              $ _
```

2. You type a command line and press the ENTER key:

```
C:\> COPI OLD NEW          $ dp old new
```

3. The system displays an error message on the screen, followed by another prompt:

```
C:\> COPI OLD NEW          $ dp old new
Bad command or file name   sh: dp: not found
C:\> _                     $ _
```

Now let's review these basic common points and differences between the two systems. Both systems present a prompt on the screen. The DOS prompt usually identifies the drive you are using; the UNIX prompt never does. The command names in the examples above are different, but the syntax is the same. There is no rule about this. Sometimes both systems use identical command names, but most of the time they use different names. The syntax is sometimes similar, but the options are never exactly the same. Error messages in the two systems, of course, are different.

DOS commands can be typed in either upper or lowercase letters. UNIX commands are always in lowercase letters. To make a clear distinction between the two in this book, all DOS commands are shown in uppercase. This way, you can recognize the DOS examples immediately, without even having to read the command name.

In recent years, designers have made advances in the area of graphical user interfaces. These interfaces, pioneered in the "personal" computer market by the Apple Macintosh, offer pictorial icons on the screen for the user to select with the aid of a mouse. Originally, neither DOS nor UNIX currently had this kind of interface, although some versions of UNIX offer windows. However, the successor to DOS, OS/2, will offer an icon-based interface, and several interfaces, such as Open Look, SunTools, and NextStep, have been developed for UNIX.

A Comparison of Commands

As illustrated in the above examples, you can carry out many of the same tasks with either system. You will find many differences in command names and command line syntax. Right now, we'll take a look at command names, which are shown in Table 1-1. Syntax is discussed in later chapters.

Table 1-1. Commands with Similar Functions

DOS Command	UNIX Command	Function
DIR	ls	List the names of files in a directory
CD	cd	Move from one directory to another
MD	mkdir	Make a new directory
RD	rmdir	Remove a directory
TYPE	cat	Display a file's contents on the screen
COPY	cp	Copy a file (or a set of files)
REN	mv	Rename a file
DEL	rm	Remove a file (or a set of files)
---	ln	Link a file
---	chmod	Change file access permissions
---	cal	Display a calendar on the screen

Table 1-1. Commands with Similar Functions (cont'd)

DOS Command	UNIX Command	Function
PRINT	**lp**	Print a file
---	**lpstat**	Display the status of printing jobs
---	**find**	Locate files by contents
SORT	**sort**	Sort a file (or set of files) by line
---	**dc**	Run the desk calculator
---	**bc**	Run the high-precision calculator
EDLIN	**ed or vi**	Perform text-editing
---	**nroff**	Format printed output for fixed-width text
---	**troff**	Format printed output for variable-width text
---	**write**	Send a message to another user
---	**calendar**	Send yourself a reminder
---	**mail**	Send a message by electronic mail
---	**cu**	Call up another computer system
---	**uucp**	Exchange files with another computer system
XCOPY	**cpio**	Perform backup and recovery of files

If you've been using DOS for some time, you probably notice that UNIX offers many functions in Table 1-1 that you find only in accessory programs to DOS. For example, the programs for displaying a calendar and running a desk calculator are not included in DOS, but are available in programs you can buy for a DOS system.

Other functions, such as electronic mail and communication with other systems, show the role of UNIX in supporting many users and connecting many systems together. In DOS, you can obtain functions like these only by paying (and paying heavily) for separate hardware and software.

Different Features

Actually, the differences between the two systems have already begun to show up. Now we'll continue to look at features that separate DOS from UNIX.

Text Processing

In DOS, if you want to produce memos, letters, reports, or manuscripts, you have to buy a word processing program like WordPerfect or Microsoft Word. The **EDLIN** program provided by DOS is too primitive for anything but the most elementary text processing tasks. In UNIX, several programs are built into the system. The visual interpreter, **vi**, provides text processing, while the **nroff** and **troff** formatters provide text formatting as a separate function.

This separation between editing and formatting represents the technology of the 1960s. All UNIX formatters require that you embed cryptic commands into your text files, to be processed at the time you print the text. Today, with the advent of programs like Aldus PageMaker and Ventura Publisher, many people may view the "edit-and-format" method used by UNIX programs as outmoded.

However, help is on the way. WordPerfect and FrameMaker are now available for UNIX systems, and more programs are sure to follow. Some day, UNIX may become as well supported by application programs as DOS is today.

Programming Accessories

People who develop software like the wide array of development tools available on UNIX systems. The UNIX command processor, also called the *shell*, includes its own complete programming language. Then there is the language in which most of UNIX itself is written, the C language, together with FORTRAN and a number of debuggers, compilers, and analyzers.

The DOS command processor also includes a programming language, but it is less extensive than the ones provided by UNIX. While DOS has its own debugger, most of the tools that people use for programming are found in outside programs. The only built-in language in DOS is BASIC, which is good for learning how to program, but is not a systems programming tool.

System Administration

Because of its complexity, each UNIX installation must have a system administrator. The responsibilities of the system administrator include setting up accounts for new users, closing down old accounts, backing up files, installing various hardware devices, formatting disks, getting rid of obsolete files, preventing unauthorized entry, and starting up and shutting down the system. UNIX provides a separate user account, a separate directory, and a separate set of commands to perform these tasks.

It is much easier to oversee a single-user DOS system. The primary tasks are formatting disks, backing up files, organizing directories, and setting up initialization files. Most DOS users can accomplish these tasks without special training, using some programs included with DOS or some outside programs.

Hardware Base

As noted above, Microsoft developed DOS specifically for the IBM PC. Of course, DOS also runs on the IBM machines introduced later, the PC/XT, the PC/AT, and on the IBM-compatible machines. DOS runs only on one small family of computers, but it happens to be the most widely used family in the industry.

UNIX was originally developed on a minicomputer, the DEC PDP-7. However, in the 20 years since its development, it has been ported to a wide variety of minicomputers, personal computers, and mainframes. And with the advent of the Motorola 68000 and Intel 80386 microprocessors, UNIX finally has microcomputers powerful enough to run it.

The Pros and Cons of UNIX

The Strengths of UNIX

On the positive side, UNIX has been around a long time. This means that it has been through many versions, and its features have stood the test of time for 20 years. Unlike OS/2, it's available right now to anyone who wants to use it.

As mentioned above, UNIX is available on many systems. This is a definite plus to any company that uses a variety of computers for different purposes. Using the same operating system on all the computers neutralizes their differences and unifies them into one large whole.

As a multiuser system, UNIX is made for teamwork and group projects. Many companies are looking for ways to connect their computers together. Those with DOS systems are turning more and more frequently to local area networks to provide this connection. However, UNIX comes with connectivity built in.

The Weaknesses of UNIX

Obviously UNIX has drawbacks. Otherwise, it would have become much more popular during the 1980s and lived up to people's expectations for it. Number one on the list is probably its user interface. A system that uses command names like **grep** and **awk** isn't going to find wide popular support among computer users. Many people already have fears about using computers even before they encounter names like these.

Another major factor has to be the lack of standardization. With DOS, there is just one system, period. With UNIX, there have been different, incompatible versions of the system for at least 10 years. The three main versions have been the AT&T versions, the Berkeley versions, and the Microsoft XENIX versions. Each one has been targeted at a different market. AT&T has sought out commercial users on minicomputers; Berkeley has appealed to researchers and engineers using workstations; XENIX has been designed for commercial users on personal computers. A recent product called System V/386, Release 3.2 merges AT&T UNIX with XENIX, but Berkeley UNIX is still incompatible.

A third factor that turns many people away from UNIX is its need for extensive system administration. Ordinary users can buy DOS and take care of it themselves. But UNIX requires full-time professional support seven days a week, and the price of neglect can be total catastrophe. If you forget to back up your DOS files or perform unfragmentation, you may be inconvenienced or you may have a messy system. But if you turn off your machine without shutting the UNIX system down properly, you run the risk of wiping out your entire system. High stakes like these leave many people apprehensive about using a UNIX system.

Conclusion

Some say that DOS and UNIX are like English and Esperanto. With all its peculiarities and limitations, English has become a universal language. In spite of its technical excellence and its potential to unify many people, Esperanto is spoken only by a tiny, dedicated minority. While its idiosyncrasies might have held it back during the 1980s, UNIX is beginning to gain momentum now. Technical workstations and multiuser systems are taking UNIX to more and more computer users.

## CHAPTER 2

BASIC PROCEDURES

Introduction

Beginning and ending a work session on a DOS system are very simple. To begin, you just turn on the machine, enter the date and time, and go to work. (If the machine has an internal clock, you don't even have to enter the date and time.) To end the session, you just exit from your application program and turn off the machine. (For systems with a hard disk, it's also a good idea to park the read/write heads before turning off the machine. But some systems park the heads automatically.)

Beginning and ending a session on a UNIX system are a little more involved. To begin for the first time, you have to take care of several administrative details (obtaining a name to identify you, obtaining a password to help protect the system, and making sure your terminal is compatible with the host computer). Then, to begin each session, you have to log into the UNIX system. To end the session, you have to log out of the system.

System Administration

In a typical UNIX system with many users, one person is usually assigned the responsibility of managing the operation of the host computer. This individual, called the *system administrator*, takes care of starting up and shutting down the host computer; connecting terminals, printers, disks, tapes, and modems; backing up files; getting new users started; protecting the system from unauthorized entry; and so on.

On a large UNIX system, system administration is often a full-time job in itself, requiring a qualified professional. A system administrator must have a knowledge of computer hardware and software, as well as the ability to work with people skillfully. This person has to maintain the system, keep it running efficiently, offer advice to users, and encourage users to cooperate with the system administrator.

On a desktop UNIX system, you may have to become your own system administrator. If so, then you will have to do more than log in and log out when you use your system. You will also have to handle system startup and shutdown. These complex tasks are discussed much later in this book; however, you should be aware of them if you are acting as your own system administrator. For the rest of this chapter, we'll assume that the UNIX system is already running and you are ready to begin work on it as an ordinary user.

Security

Names for users and passwords are aids in maintaining security. Computer systems attract people the way trout attract fishermen. Some people spend a great deal of time figuring out ways to enter computer systems. Most of them are just curious. But unfortunately, a few of them break into computer systems to pillage and plunder.

System administrators and ordinary UNIX users have to work together as a team to prevent outsiders from entering their systems. Security begins with the use of passwords. Each user has to consider more than the "inconvenience" of using a password. File access permissions also help protect the system.

Preview

In the rest of this chapter, we'll go through the following procedures:

- Preliminary steps
- Logging in
- Entering commands
- Changing your password
- Logging out

Preliminary Steps _____

Obtaining a Login Name

It is the responsibility of the system administrator to assign a login name to each user of the system. You can request your first name, last name, nickname, initials, or anything else you can remember easily. Although you are allowed up to 14 characters, you will probably want to keep your login name shorter.

If your name is Robert K. Anderson, you may want to use one of the following as a login name:

- robert
- bob
- rka
- anderson
- robta

Each system administrator keeps a record of the names of authorized users. Once assigned, your name is stored and checked each time you log in.

Obtaining a Password

The system administrator assigns a password along with each login name. The usual procedure is to assign a temporary password, with the understanding that the user will immediately change it to something more appropriate. For example, for Robert K. Anderson, a system administrator could assign these names:

```
Login name:    robert
Password:      anderson
```

A password can be up to 14 characters long, and the longer, the better. You should try to use as many different kinds of characters as possible (uppercase and lowercase letters, numbers, and symbols). Here are a few suggestions for passwords that are easy to remember, yet difficult for intruders to guess:

```
•  EZ_2_remember.        14 characters
•  Why_not_today?        14 characters
•  Let's_try_it!         13 characters
```

On some systems, each user is required to change passwords periodically. On others, every password must be at least six characters long. Even if your system doesn't require it, use a longer password and change it from time to time. Your UNIX system will be safer.

Setting Up Your Terminal

Most users of a UNIX system access the host computer through a terminal. A *terminal* is a machine that allows you to communicate with a computer both ways (entering input and receiving output). In today's world, input is via an electronic keyboard and output is via a video monitor. (If you are using a desktop system, the terminal is built into the computer, and you don't have to do anything about it.)

In the most typical UNIX configuration, many terminals are connected to a host computer (see Figure 2-1). Each terminal must be set to match the communication settings of the host. This means making sure that terminal and host are both sending and receiving at the same speed, using the same units, employing the same error detection scheme, and following the same protocol. The key words are

- speed
- word length
- parity
- protocol

The way to find out whether your terminal is set correctly is to attempt to log in (as described in the next section) and see what happens. If your screen displays double characters, no characters, random characters, or no response when you press ENTER, then you will have to change the settings. Either you or your system administrator will have to use the **stty** command, which is described in Chapter 14, "Managing Terminals."

Completing A Session

Logging In

With a login name, a password, and a terminal that is set up correctly, you can log in and go to work. The steps, which may vary from one system to another, are

1. Establish connection:
   a. Connect your terminal to the host computer by doing one of the following:
      - Dial the computer through your modem
      - Type something at your keyboard
      - Flip a switch on your terminal
   b. The system will display the following prompt:

   ```
   login:
   ```

2. Identify yourself:
   a. Type your login name and press ENTER (or RETURN).
   b. The system will display the prompt:

   ```
   Password: _
   ```

3. Enter your password:

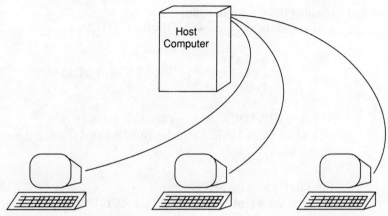

Figure 2-1. A Typical UNIX System

    a. Type your password, which will not be displayed on the
       screen, and press ENTER (or RETURN).
    b. The system will display something like this:

```
Last login: Fri Feb 23  09:12:56  on tty05
UNIX System V, Release 3.2
$ _
```

The dollar sign ($) lets you know that the UNIX system is ready for you to
enter a command. The actual symbol that you see may be a dollar sign ($), a
percent sign (%), or a pound sign (#), as you will learn later in this book. This
symbol, called the UNIX *shell* prompt, corresponds to the DOS prompt:

```
C:\> _
```

In DOS, the prompt for entering a command includes the name of the current disk drive (C:) and possibly the name of the current directory. In UNIX,
references to drive names are rare, and the shell prompt never includes such
information.

Entering Commands

Once you have logged in, you can begin using the UNIX system, which means
entering commands. Entering commands is about the same whether you are
using DOS or UNIX. The only difference is that most UNIX commands have
different names. Here are some examples:

1. Display the date and time:
   a. Type **date** and press ENTER (or RETURN):

   ```
   $ date
   Fri Feb 23 09:17:34 PST 1991
   $ _
   ```

   b. Like DOS, UNIX displays another prompt ($).
   c. Unlike DOS, UNIX includes the date and time in the same command.

2. Find out who else is logged in:
   a. Type **who** and press ENTER (or RETURN):

   ```
   $ who
   val         tty01       Feb 23    08:21
   jane        tty02       Feb 23    08:49
   bill        tty05       Feb 23    09:12
   ted         tty08       Feb 23    08:36
   pbr         tty11       Feb 22    18:07
   toad        tty12       Feb 23    08:58
   $ _
   ```

   b. The display for **who** includes this information on each user currently logged in:

   - Login name
   - Terminal name (ttynnn)
   - Date and time of login

   In the late 1960s when UNIX had its beginnings, it was common to use a printing Teletype machine as a terminal. This is why the letters **tty** are used to identify terminals in a UNIX system.

3. Enter a non-UNIX command:
   a. Type **what** and press ENTER (or RETURN):

   ```
   $ what
   sh: what: not found
   $ _
   ```

   b. Since there is no UNIX command called **what**, the system displays an error message, just as DOS would.

Changing Your Password

At first, the system administrator will probably **assign** you a login name and a temporary password (your last name, for **example**). As soon as you log in, you should change your password to something **more** suitable. On some systems, you may be required to change your **password** periodically (for example, at the beginning of each month). Here is an **example**:

1. Request a change of passwords:
   a. Type **passwd** and press ENTER (or RETURN):

   ```
   $ passwd
   Changing old password for bill
   Old password: _
   ```

   b. Type your present password and press ENTER (or RETURN).

2. Make the change:
   a. Enter your new password:

   ```
   New password: _
   ```

   b. Enter your new password again:

   ```
   Retype your new password: _
   $ _
   ```

   Guidelines for selecting a suitable password **were** given earlier in this chapter.

Entering a Command Line

Earlier in this chapter, you entered **simple** commands by themselves, such as **date**, **who**, and **passwd**. UNIX commands, like DOS commands, can also be entered with *arguments*. In DOS, you use a slash (/) to introduce an argument. For example, to format the disk in drive B and copy the system to the disk, you would use this DOS command:

```
C:\> FORMAT B: /S
```

In UNIX, you usually use a minus sign (−) to introduce an argument. However, sometimes you use a plus sign (+), and sometimes you don't use anything. For example, one form of the **who** command can be used to determine your own login name. You can use this when you are working on more than one terminal at a time and you are unsure of your current login name:

```
$ who am i
bill        tty05      Feb 23   09:12
$ _
```

You will learn a great deal more about arguments in the rest of the book. For now, it is enough to be aware of their existence. In the example above, the argument **am i** modifies the basic command **who**.

When you are entering a command line, with or without arguments, it may be helpful to know the key combinations for editing the line. To erase one character, press one of these:

- # (the pound sign)
- CTRL H (hold down the CTRL key and press H (or h)
- BACKSPACE (a separate key on many keyboards)

Your system should be set up to accept one or more of these keys. Here is an example of erasing the previous character on the command line (using # as the erase key):

```
$ whom          [You type m accidentally]
$ who           [Press # to erase the m]
$ who           [Press ENTER to execute the command]
Fri Feb 23 09:23 PST 1991
$ _
```

To erase an entire command line, press one of these:

- @ (at sign in UNIX)
- CTRL U (in XENIX)

Here is an example of clearing a command line and starting over (using @ as the kill key):

```
$ qho am i      [You type q by mistake]
$ qho am i      [Press @ to erase the entire line]
who am i        [Retype the command line and press ENTER]
bill      tty05      Feb 23   09:12
$ _
```

When you press the kill key (@), you probably won't see the command line erased. Instead, you will see the cursor drop down to the next line without a shell prompt. Then you can retype the command line there.

There may be times when you enter a command and nothing happens. You get no output and no shell prompt appears. In this situation, you can press DEL to restore the prompt. For example:

```
$ who              [You enter a command; nothing happens]
_                  [Press DEL to restore the prompt]
$ _                [The prompt returns]
```

A command running under either DOS or UNIX may generate more lines of output than your screen can display at once. Under either operating system, you can halt a scrolling display by pressing CTRL S (holding down CTRL and pressing S). To resume scrolling after viewing the screen, press CTRL Q.

Logging Out

At the end of each session on a UNIX system, you have to log out. You can't just turn off your terminal and walk away. You will still be considered logged in, and you may have to pay for extra time on the system.

On most systems, you log out by pressing CTRL D (holding down CTRL and pressing D (or d)). After you've logged out, the login prompt returns to the screen, as shown here:

```
$ -                [Press CTRL D to log out; nothing is
                   displayed]
login: _           [The login prompt appears]
```

On some systems, you may be required to type logout, as shown here:

```
$ logout           [Enter logout instead of CTRL D]
login: _           [The login prompt appears]
```

No matter how you log out, make sure the login prompts appears. Otherwise, you haven't logged out.

Brady Books
15 Columbus Circle
New York, NY 10023

## CHAPTER 3

FILES AND DIRECTORIES

Disks and Diskettes

DOS Conventions

When you're using DOS, you have to be aware of disk and diskette drives, and you have to use drive names when you execute commands. For example, if the current drive is C and you want to copy a file to a diskette in drive A, you have to use a command like this:

```
C:\> COPY TEST A:
```

If the file you are copying resides on a diskette in yet another drive, you also have to name that drive. For example, if the file is on drive B instead of the current drive, you have to enter the command shown above as follows:

```
C:\> COPY B:TEST A:
```

In DOS, drives A and B are set aside for diskettes, while drives C, D, E, and so on are intended for hard disks. Each drive has its own separate directory tree, as illustrated in Figure 3-1.

The simple DOS system shown in Figure 3-1 has a 5.25-inch diskette drive called A, a 3.5-inch diskette drive called B, and a hard disk called C. Each

A:\	B:\	C:\
A:\INTRO	B:\TM401	C:\SYSTEM
A:\TEXT	B:\TM402	C:\PROGRAMS
	B:\TM403	C:\PROJECTS
		C:\PLANNING

Figure 3-1. A DOS System with Three Drives

disk (or diskette) has its own root directory, with different subdirectories under each. Each directory tree can have its own structure, with subdirectories going down several more levels than shown in Figure 3-1. But the structure shown is detailed enough to illustrate the relationship between drives and directory names.

UNIX Conventions

In UNIX, references to drive names are rare. Except for a few XENIX commands for transferring files back and forth between DOS and XENIX, drive names are not used. This is because drives are *mounted* on a UNIX system (that is, integrated into the system). When you use UNIX commands, you still have to refer to directories, but not to drives. Drives appear in a UNIX system under directory names and are known to users only as directories, not as drives. Unless you are a system administrator performing administrative tasks, you don't have to be aware of drives or drive names.

Another difference between DOS and UNIX is that the major directory names in a UNIX system are more or less fixed. While there may be some variations from system to system, a UNIX system typically includes one root directory with five major directories under the root directory, which are listed in Table 3-1.

Table 3-1. The Major Directories of UNIX

Name	Contents
usr	Login directories for system users
bin	Binary files (programs)
tmp	Temporary files
dev	Device files
etc	Administrative files

All this must be completely new to someone who has used only DOS. While it may be helpful for a DOS user to set up separate directories for programs, administration, and day-to-day work, it certainly isn't required. DOS allows you to use any directory names you choose. But the naming requirements under UNIX don't stop with the major directories. Many files used by the UNIX system have to reside in particular directories.

Each time you log into a UNIX system, you find yourself in the same directory. This directory, known as your HOME DIRECTORY, will probably be a subdirectory of major directory USR. Your login name will probably be the same as the name of your home directory. After you've logged in, you can move to other directories. But you always start each session in your home directory.

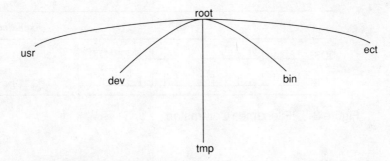

Figure 3-2. A Typical UNIX File System

While the standard name for the directory that contains users' home directories is **usr**, sometimes its name is **U**, **USR1**, **USR2**, or something else. On very large systems with many users, there may be more than one such directory, with some home directories in one directory and others in another.

A typical UNIX system is shown in Figure 3-2.

Hardware Devices

In DOS, hardware devices are identified by abbreviations that sometimes end with colons (:). For example, disk drives, as mentioned earlier, are called A:, B:, C:, and so on. The serial ports are called COM1, COM2, and so on. The parallel ports are called LPT1, LPT2, and so on. The console (keyboard and video display) is called CON, and the printer is called PRN.

In UNIX, hardware devices are identified in a completely different way. Directory **dev**, mentioned earlier in this chapter, contains files that represent hardware devices. These files, called *special files*, can be used like the DOS abbreviations to refer to hardware devices.

Naming Conventions

Now we'll discuss the difference between naming DOS files and UNIX files. In DOS, the root directory is identified by a backslash (\), which is also used to separate the name of each directory in the hierarchy from the name of each of its subdirectories. You can use up to eight characters for the base name of each file; then you have the option of adding a period (.) and up to three more characters to form an extension. You are allowed to use letters, numbers, and most symbols (excluding periods, commas, question marks, asterisks, slashes, and backslashes). Finally, DOS is not case-sensitive, which means that it doesn't matter whether you type letters in upper- or lowercase.

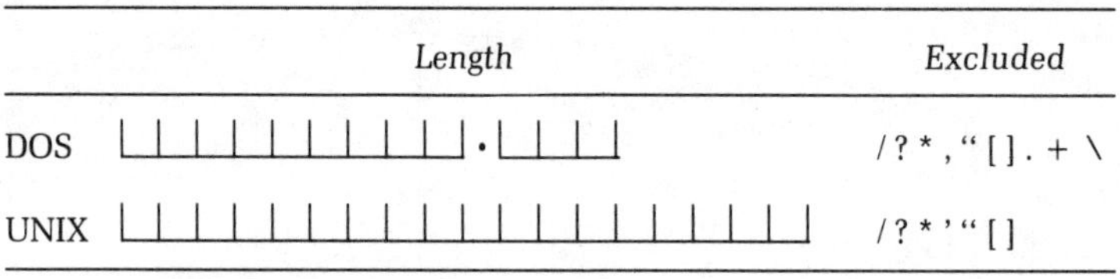
Length
Excluded
DOS
/ ? * , “ [ ] . + \
UNIX
/ ? * ’ “ [ ]

Figure 3-3. Filenames Contrasted

In UNIX, the root directory is identified by a slash (/), which also separates directory names from each other. You can use up to 14 characters, including letters, numbers, and symbols other than slashes, question marks, asterisks, quotation marks, and brackets. You can use a period anywhere in a UNIX filename, and UNIX is case-sensitive, which means that it distinguishes between a filename in uppercase letters and the same name in lowercase letters.

The differences between DOS and UNIX filenames are shown graphically in Figure 3-3.

Suppose you have a UNIX file named **memo** that belongs to user **paul**. That is, the file is in a directory named **paul**, which is a subdirectory of **usr**. The full name (or *pathname*) of the file would be **/usr/paul/memo.** If you were to create a file by the same name on a DOS disk in drive A that happened to contain the same directory names, the full name of the file in DOS would be **a:\usr\paul\memo** (or **A:\USR\PAUL\MEMO**).

The two names are nearly identical. The only differences are that the UNIX name uses slashes instead of backslashes, the UNIX name is not preceded by a disk name, and the UNIX name must remain lowercase. The reason the two names are so similar, of course, is that the naming conventions for DOS were derived from those for UNIX. As soon as DOS began supporting directories, the designers adopted the UNIX naming conventions (with some modifications).

Most DOS filenames are valid in UNIX, but the converse is definitely not true. Here are some examples of valid filenames in UNIX that would never be valid in DOS:

```
old.report
3rd.week+month
stock.prices
old+new.rates
```

In both operating systems, one period (.) is used to represent the current directory and two periods (..) are used to represent the parent directory (the directory that is above the current directory).

File Types

In DOS, you can use certain specified extension names to identify certain types of files. For example, batch files are identified by the extension **.BAT**. These extensions are listed in Table 3-2.

Table 3-2. Some File Extensions Used by DOS

Extension	Type of File
.ASM	A program written in assembly language, a symbolic programming language that is close to machine code.
.BAS	A program written in BASIC, a common programming language.
.BAT	A batch file, which contains a sequence of DOS commands to be executed.
.COM	A command file (a file that contains an executable program); similar to an executable file.
.EXE	An executable file (a file that contains an executable program); similar to a command file.
.SYS	A DOS system file, which DOS uses for its own purposes.

All the kinds of files listed in Table 3-2 can also be used in a UNIX system, but the type is not indicated in the name. You may want to use some kind of designator to tell you what kind of file you have created, but the UNIX system doesn't always require it. Filename designators are used in UNIX mainly by compilers to identify those that contain source code for a particular programming language, as shown in Table 3-3.

Table 3-3. Some File Designators Used by UNIX

Symbol	Meaning
.a	File contains source code for assembly language program.
.c	File contains source code for C language program.
.f	File contains source code for FORTRAN language program.
.p	File contains source code for Pascal language program.

For example, if you wrote a UNIX test program called **test** in assembly language, you would have to call it **test.a**. If you wrote the program in C, you would call it **test.c**, and so on. However, a UNIX program file that is ready to execute does not require any special suffix like the DOS **.COM** or **.EXE**. Executability of a UNIX file is determined not by a suffix, but by a system of access permissions, which is discussed later in this chapter.

Working with Directories _____

In this section you will learn how to work with UNIX directories. Many of the commands are the same in DOS and UNIX; others are similar.

Looking at Directories

The DOS command for displaying a directory is DIR. When you use this command, you see a display that shows the name of each file, its size, and date and time of last modification. In its basic form, the UNIX ls (list) command shows only filenames: as

```
$ ls
addendum
balance
call-125
deadline
end.odd
first
$ _
```

To see a display that is more like the DOS DIR display, you have to include the −l (long) option with the **ls** command, as shown below:

```
$ ls -l
-rwxr-----  1  bill    6782  Feb  3  10:54  addendum
drwx--x---  1  bill     367  Mar 15  08:37  balance
-rw-r--r--  2  bill    9285  Apr 22  15:21  call-125
drwx------  1  bill     294  Jan 18  11:46  deadline
-rwxrw----  1  bill    8349  Dec 17  08:59  end.odd
-rw-rw-rw-  5  bill    7956  May 24  10:03  first
$ _
```

The long display includes seven columns, which are identified in Figure 3-4.

Aside from order, the last four columns are nearly identical to their counterparts in the DOS DIR listing. So we'll focus on the first four columns: type of file, access permissions, number of *links*, and owner. The very first character on each line of a long listing tells you whether the file is an ordinary file (-) or a directory (d). The **d** shown in the UNIX long listing corresponds to the <DIR> shown in the DOS DIR listing.

The next nine characters in the UNIX long listing tell you who is allowed to access your file. Access permissions are discussed in detail later in this chapter.

Linking is also discussed later in this chapter. The next number in the long listing tells you how many links there are to your file.

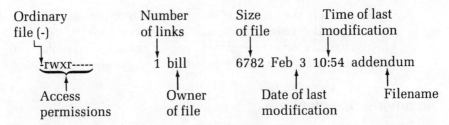

Figure 3-4. File Information in a Long Listing

Finally, the owner of the file is the user who created the file. If you are displaying files in your home directory, you should see your own login name here.

Changing Directories

The command for changing directories is the same for DOS and UNIX: **cd** (change directories). In DOS, you can include the name of the current working directory in your DOS prompt. Since you can't do this in UNIX, there is a UNIX command for displaying the name of the current directory: **pwd** (print working directory). Here is an example of using **pwd**:

```
$ pwd
/usr/paul/memos
$ cd ../letters
$ pwd
/usr/paul/letters
$ _
```

This is probably a good time to explain the use of the word *print* in the UNIX system. Since the terminals used when UNIX had its beginnings were printing Teletype machines, print meant display. To the contemporary video display user, printing means displaying on your screen. The UNIX terminology has remained the same, even though the technology has changed.

Creating a Directory

The UNIX **mkdir** (make directory) command is just like the DOS MD command. Here is an example:

```
$ pwd
/usr/paul
$ mkdir news
$ _
```

The effect of the command shown above is to create a new subdirectory of **/usr/paul** called **news** (that is, **/usr/paul/news**). To work most effectively, you should have a moderate number of primary directories (about 5–20), with your subdirectories evenly distributed within your primary directories.

Removing Directories

The UNIX **rmdir** (remove directory) command is similar to the DOS RD command. Before you can remove a directory, you have to delete all the files in the directory. Then the simplest method is to move to the parent to delete the directory. For example, here is how you would delete **/usr/paul/letters**:

```
$ cd ..
$ pwd
/usr/paul
$ rmdir letters
$ _
```

If the directory is empty (that is, contains no files), it will be removed and will no longer appear in directory listings.

Renaming a Directory

The Norton Utilities allow you to rename a DOS directory, but DOS itself does not. However, you can rename a UNIX directory with the **mv** (move) command. For example, to change the name of a subdirectory of the current directory from **ancient** to **modern**, use the following command:

```
$ mv ancient modern
$ _
```

The name of the directory will be changed from **ancient** to **modern**, with the same owner and access permissions.

Working with Files

Any time you use a computer, you are working with files. Files are used to contain text, spreadsheets, databases, programs, and information about the computer system. It's essential to know how to create new files, delete old files, and copy and move files from directory to directory.

Examining Files

The UNIX **cat** (concatenate) command can be used like the DOS TYPE command to display the contents of a file on the screen. Here is an example:

```
$ cat reminder
Reminder: The next
department meeting
will be Wednesday
at 10:00.
$ _
```

If the file doesn't exist (or if you misspell it), you will see a message like the following:

```
$ cat remainder
cat: cannot open remainder
$ _
```

Concatenation, the other main function of the **cat** command, will be discussed in the next chapter.

Copying Files

The UNIX **cp** (copy) command is similar to the DOS COPY command. In its simplest form, **cp** makes a copy of one file in the same directory, as shown here:

```
$ cp old.report new.report
$ _
```

You can also copy a file to another directory, with or without a new name. Here is an example of copying to another directory and renaming at the same time. In the example below, file **old.report** will be copied to directory **reports** and renamed **new.report**:

```
$ cp old.report ../reports/new.report
$ _
```

The UNIX **cp** command can also be used to copy more than one file at a time. In the example that follows, three files will be copied to another with their names retained:

```
$ cp amber berry catch ../memos
$ _
```

Note that the UNIX **cp** doesn't list the names of the files being copied, as the DOS COPY command does.

Moving and Renaming Files

The UNIX **mv** (move) command can be used either to move files to another directory or to rename them. You can also move and rename files simultaneously. To move a file to another directory without renaming it, you can use a command line like the following:

```
$ mv memo-027 ../memos
$ _
```

To move the same file and also rename it **minutes**, you can use this command line:

```
$ mv memo-027 ../memos/minutes
$ _
```

The **mv** command, like the **cp** command, allows you to move more than one file at once. Here is an example, with **ls** used to confirm the move:

```
$ mv memo-001 memo-002 memo-003 ../memos
$ ls ../memos
. . .
memo-001
memo-002
memo-003
. . .
$ _
```

When used to rename files, the UNIX **mv** command is like the DOS REN (rename) command. In the following example, we'll check to make sure the target name doesn't already exist and then change the name of file **old.memo** to **new.memo**:

```
$ ls new.memo
$ mv old.memo new.memo
$ _
```

The **ls** command is used in the preceding example to avoid overwriting a file that may already be called **new.memo**. The absence of output indicates that there is no file by that name, meaning that you can use that name.

Deleting Files

The UNIX **rm** (remove) command corresponds to the DOS DEL command. In the next example, we'll delete three files from the current directory:

```
$ rm memo.1 memo.2 memo.3
$ _
```

When you use **rm** in its basic form, as shown above, the files named are deleted immediately. You don't have a chance to confirm the deletions one at a time. If you'd like to confirm each deletion before it is carried out, you can include the **-i** (interactive) option, as shown in this example:

```
$ rm -i memo.1 memo.2 memo.3
memo.1: ?
memo.2: ?
memo.3: ?
$ _
```

In the interactive example above, you will see the name of each file displayed one at a time. Then you can type either **y** (yes) to confirm the deletion or **n** (no) to prevent the deletion.

Linking Files

Giving each user a private home directory is good for UNIX security. But what if several users have to share the same file? Then each user can have a *link* to the file (that is, another name for the file in another directory). There is still only one file, but each link makes that file accessible to another user.

For example, consider the following: Bob and Ray are both working on a project that involves the use of file **cobra**; file **cobra** resides in Ray's directory **plans**; Bob wants to be able to work on file **cobra** without leaving his home directory. Once Ray gives Bob permission to access file **cobra**, Bob can execute the following **ln** command line from directory **projects**. Then he will be able to access file **cobra** from his own **projects** directory.

```
$ pwd
/usr/bob/projects
$ ln /usr/ray/plans/cobra cobra
$ _
```

Now Bob can access the file and make changes to it. The next time Ray accesses the file, he will see the changes made by Bob. If Ray makes changes to the file, Bob will see them the next time he accesses the file. In addition,

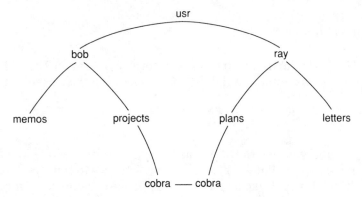

Figure 3-5. A Link Illustrated

after Bob has executed the above command line, one more link is added to the long listing display. The link is shown graphically in Figure 3-5.

Note that Bob could have given the file a different name when he executed the **ln** command line. If he wanted to call the file **snake**, he could have used the following command line:

```
$ ln /usr/ray/plans/cobra snake
$ _
```

Any user who has a link to a given file can delete it. As long as other links remain, the original file will remain. Only one link will be removed. For example, if Bob called his link **cobra**, he can remove it with a sequence like this:

```
$ pwd
/usr/bob/projects
$ rm cobra
$ _
```

Matching Characters

DOS and UNIX both use the wildcard characters **?** and * to match either a single character (?) or any number of characters (*). But UNIX has an additional method for matching characters. You can enter specific characters between a pair of brackets. For example, suppose you have the following nine files:

```
memo.a        memo.b        memo.c
memo.d        memo.e        memo.f
memo.g        memo.h        memo.i
```

To delete the three files in the second column, you can use this UNIX command line:

```
$ rm memo.[beh]
$ _
```

The command line shown just above is equivalent to the following:

```
$ rm memo.b memo.e memo.h
$ _
```

To copy the three files in the second row, you can use this command line:

```
$ cp memo.[def]
$ _
```

The above command line is equivalent to the following:

```
$ cp memo.d memo.e memo.f
$ _
```

File Permissions

A UNIX system administrator is responsible for maintaining system security. One way to do this is to restrict file access using a system of file permissions. These permissions determine which users can and cannot use a given file. Permissions apply to the owner, others who may belong to the owner's working group, and all other users.

In the paragraphs that follow, we'll begin with reading the notation for permissions in the long listing. Then we'll discuss how you can change permissions. The concepts described in this section have no counterpart in DOS.

Reading Permissions

You learned about the **ls** command's long listing earlier in this chapter. Here is an example:

```
$ ls -l
-rwxr-----  1  bill     6782  Feb  3  10:54  addendum
drwx--x---  1  bill      367  Mar 15  08:37  balance
-rw-r--r--  2  bill     9285  Apr 22  15:21  call-125
drwx------  1  bill      294  Jan 18  11:46  deadline
-rwxrw----  1  bill     8349  Dec 17  08:59  end+odd
-rw-rw-rw-  5  bill     7956  May 24  10:03  first
$ _
```

The first column contains 10 characters. As noted earlier in this chapter, the first character indicates the type of file:

-    Ordinary file
- d   Directory

The nine characters that follow symbolize the permissions that apply to the file. Although there are no spaces separating them, the nine characters represent three columns of three characters each. The first column symbolizes permissions for the owner (or user), the second column shows those for the owner's working group (if the user belongs to one), and the third column shows those for all other users on the system.

If we could take the 10 characters of the first column and spread them out for easier viewing, they would look something like this:

Type	User	Group	Others	Name
-	rwx	r--	---	addendum
d	rwx	--x	---	balance
-	rw-	r--	r--	call-125
d	rwx	---	---	deadline
-	rwx	rw-	---	end.odd
-	rw-	rw-	rw-	first

Under each of the permission columns (User, Group, Others), you find three characters. These symbolize permission to read (**r**), permission to write (**w**), permission to execute (**x**), and permission denied (−). These permissions differ somewhat in meaning for ordinary files and directories, as shown in Table 3-4.

Table 3-4. Permissions Interpreted

Permission	Meaning for a File	Meaning for a Directory
Read	View the contents	View the files
Write	Change the contents	Add files to and remove files from the directory
Execute	Execute as a command	Change to the directory, search it, and copy files from it

Suppose we select a line from the long listing and take a closer look at its permissions:

```
-          rwx        rw-        ---        end.odd
```

The nine permission symbols can be interpreted as follows:

The owner of **end.odd** can

r   read the file
w   write to it
x   execute it as a command

Members of the owner's working group can

r   read the file
w   write to it
-    not execute it

All other users are denied access:

-    no reading
-    no writing
-    no executing

The third permission (**x**), as applied to an ordinary file, allows you to execute a program as a UNIX command. An executable UNIX file corresponds to a DOS file that has a suffix of either **.COM** or **.EXE**. A UNIX file requires only execute permission; it doesn't have to include any particular suffix.

Changing Permissions

To change permissions for any file that you own, you can use the **chmod** (change [access] mode) command. With this command, you can use the three symbols already described, along with symbols for adding permissions (**+**), removing permissions (**−**), or assigning permissions absolutely (**=**). Absolute assignment of permissions means replacing all existing permissions with a new set. Finally, you have symbols to represent the owner (**u**), the working group (**g**), other users (**o**), and all users (**a**).

For example, suppose you wanted to grant read permission to other users for the file just described. Then you could execute the following command line:

```
$ chmod o+r end.odd
$ _
```

The name of the command comes first (**chmod**), then the permission(s) granted or denied (**o+r**), then the name of the file (**end.odd**). The command line shown above adds (**+**) permission to read (**r**) to other users (**o**). The name of the file always follows the assignment of permissions.

The symbols that you can use in a **chmod** command are summarized in Table 3-5. For each command line, you have to choose one symbol from the first column, one from the second, and at least one from the third.

Table 3-5. Symbols for Permissions.

Users		Action		Permission	
u	owner (user)	+	add permission	r	to read
g	group	–	remove permission	w	to write
o	others	=	absolute permission	x	to execute
a	all users (default)				

If you want to change permissions for more than one set of users, you can include more than one change in your command line. All you have to do is separate changes with commas (with no spaces). For example, to add execute permission for your working group and read and write permission for other users, execute this command:

```
$ chmod g+x,o+wx call-125
$ _
```

To see the changes while you are making them, use the **ls −l** command before and after each **chmod** command line. To restrict the long listing display to a single file, include the name of the file in the **ls** command line. Here is an example:

```
$ ls -l call-125
-rw-r--r-- 2  bill      9285  Apr 22  15:21  call-125
$ chmod g+x,o+wx call-125
$ ls -l call-125
-rw-r-xrwx 2  bill      9285  Apr 22  15:21  call-125
$ _
```

To revoke permissions, use a minus sign instead of a plus sign. The following example shows how you could revoke the permissions that you just granted in the previous example:

```
$ ls -l call-125
-rw-r-xrwx 2  bill      9285  Apr 22  15:21  call-125
$ chmod g-x,o-wx call-125
$ ls -l call-125
-rw-r--r-- 2  bill      9285  Apr 22  15:21  call-125
$ _
```

You can also grant or revoke permissions by clearing all permissions currently in effect and setting new ones using an equal sign (=). For example, suppose you want to revoke all permissions for **call − 125** and assign the following new ones: read and write permission for yourself, read permission for your group, and read permission for others. Here's the command line:

```
$ ls -l call-125
-rw-r-xrwx  2  bill        9285  Apr 22  15:21  call-125
$ chmod u=rw,g=r,o=r call-125
$ ls -l call-125
-rw-r--r--  2  bill        9285  Apr 22  15:21  call-125
$ _
```

NOTE: Be careful when you use the **chmod** command. You can lock yourself out of your own files if you make a mistake.

## CHAPTER 4

COMMAND PROCESSING

Command Processors

A key program in any operating system is the command processor. This program takes each command line that you enter, interprets it, and carries out its execution on the system. If you make a mistake, the command processor displays an error message to help you correct it.

DOS Command Processors

The original DOS command processor, stored in a file called **COMMAND.COM**, is the one that most users are familiar with. It has grown larger and larger with each new release of DOS, adding more options and features. This command processor accepts internal commands like DIR and COPY and external commands like FORMAT and DISKCOPY, which you enter on a command line after the DOS prompt. Suppose you enter the following command line:

```
C:\> FORMAT A:/S/V
```

The command processor interprets **A:** to mean "drive A;" **/S** to mean, "Copy the system to the disk while formatting it;" and **/V** to mean, "Prompt for a volume name."

Newer releases of DOS have borrowed from UNIX other command-processing features, such as redirection and pipes. DOS now allows you to redirect a directory listing to your printer, using a command like

```
C:\> DIR > PRN
```

which the command processor interprets to mean, "Make a list of the files in the current directory and send the list to the printer instead of the screen."

As another example, DOS allows you to send output to another command through a pipe, so that the output of the first command becomes the input of the second. Here is a sample:

```
C:\> DIR : SORT
```

The command processor interprets the command line just shown to mean, "Make a list of the files in the current directory and sort the list (alphabetize the filenames)."

Version 4 of DOS also includes a visual display program that replaces command lines with window displays and menu selections. This program, called the *DOS shell*, similar to the Visual Shell supported by XENIX, but is nothing like the standard UNIX shell.

UNIX Command Processors

The original UNIX command processor, known as the *Bourne shell*, was developed at AT&T Bell Laboratories in the early 1970s by Stephen R. Bourne. This is the official UNIX shell and also the fastest-running.

Another command processor, known as the *C shell*, was developed by William Joy and others at the University of California in the mid-1970s. Borrowing many features from the C language, the C shell is more versatile than the Bourne shell, but not as fast. While the C shell is not the official command processor, it is usually available on most UNIX systems

A third command processor, called the *Korn shell*, was developed by David Korn in the early 1980s. The Korn shell, which combines many of the best features of the Bourne and C shells, is becoming more and more widely used every year. AT&T may adopt the Korn shell as its standard UNIX shell in the 1990s.

When you request a login account on a UNIX system, the system administrator will probably ask you which shell you want to use. If you are concerned about compatibility and standardization, ask for the Bourne shell. If you want to have the most powerful and convenient features, ask for the C shell. (The Korn shell is not available on the majority of UNIX systems.)

Most of the features described in this chapter are supported by all the different command processors. One way to distinguish the Bourne shell from the C shell is to notice what your screen prompt looks like. Each one uses a different symbol, as shown here:

```
Bourne shell                        C shell
$ _                                 % _
```

Commands and Arguments _____

The Shell Prompt

Any time you log into a UNIX system, the command processor (or shell) displays a prompt on the screen:

$$\$ \_ \qquad\qquad or \qquad\qquad \% \_$$

This *shell prompt*, which is like the DOS prompt C:\ >, tells you the shell is ready for you to enter a *command line*. Like a DOS command line, a UNIX command always includes a command name and may also include command options or filenames or both. Here is the general form of a UNIX command line:

$$\$ \textit{command [option(s)] [filename(s)]}$$

As in DOS, only the UNIX command name is required; one or more options may or may not be included, and one or more filenames may or may not be included. One difference to note: on a DOS command line, options (if any) are usually placed last; on a UNIX command line, options (if any) are usually placed between the command name and any filenames.

Entering a Command Line

There are four possible ways you can enter a command line for the **ls** command. First, you can enter a command line that contains only the command name, without options or filenames, as shown here:

```
$ ls
addendum
balance
call-125
deadline
end.odd
first
$ _
```

Second, you can also include an option like −**l** (long listing), as in the following example:

```
$ ls -l
total 13
-rwxr------  1  bill       6782  Feb  3  10:54  addendum
drwx--x---  1  bill        367  Mar 15  08:37  balance
```

```
-rw-r--r--   2   bill        9285   Apr 22   15:21   call-125
drwx------   1   bill         294   Jan 18   11:46   deadline
-rwxrw----   1   bill        8349   Dec 17   08:59   end.odd
-rw-rw-rw-   5   bill        7956   May 24   10:03   first
$ _
```

Third, when executing from a different directory, you can include the name of a directory (which is a filename), as illustrated here:

```
$ ls /usr/paul/memos
addendum
balance
call-125
deadline
end.odd
first
$ _
```

Fourth, when executing from a different directory, you can include an option and a directory name on the same command line, as shown below:

```
$ ls -l /usr/paul/memos
total 13
-rwxr-----   1   bill        6782   Feb  3   10:54   addendum
drwx--x---   1   bill         367   Mar 15   08:37   balance
-rw-r--r--   2   bill        9285   Apr 22   15:21   call-125
drwx------   1   bill         294   Jan 18   11:46   deadline
-rwxrw----   1   bill        8349   Dec 17   08:59   end.odd
-rw-rw-rw-   5   bill        7956   May 24   10:03   first
$ _
```

Except for the order of elements on the command line, the four examples just shown above correspond to similar examples of DOS command lines.

Arguments

In the examples given above, the −l option and the filename are collectively termed *arguments* to the **ls** command. Arguments modify the way a command works. UNIX commands generally support more arguments than DOS commands. For example, the −l option is one of 22 **ls** options. Some of the others include −r (list in reverse order), −s (sort by size), −t (sort by time of last modification), and −u (sort by time of last access).

As mentioned in the previous chapter, UNIX command options are usually preceded by hyphens, or minus signs (−). (In DOS, a slash (/) is used to introduce an option.) If you want to use more than one option, you can either type the two separately or you can type them together after the same minus sign. Typing them together is called *bundling* the options. In the following, two options (−l and −r) are bundled on a command line for the **ls** command:

```
$ ls -lr
total 13
-rw-rw-rw-   5   bill       7956   May 24   10:03   first
-rwxrw----   1   bill       8349   Dec 17   08:59   end.odd
drwx------   1   bill        294   Jan 18   11:46   deadline
-rw-r--r--   2   bill       9285   Apr 22   15:21   call-125
drwx--x---   1   bill        367   Mar 15   08:37   balance
-rwxr-----   1   bill       6782   Feb  3   10:54   addendum
$ _
```

Unfortunately, there is no consistent rule about bundling. Some UNIX commands support it and some don't. In either case, you can type the options in any order.

Commands and Processes

Since DOS is a single-tasking system, it allows only one processing activity at a time. One of the largest distinctions between the two operating systems is that UNIX is *multitasking*, meaning that it allows many tasks to go on simultaneously. Each time you execute a UNIX command, the result is a *process*. There can be many processes started from the same UNIX command. For example, if six different users on a UNIX system execute **ls** at the same time, there will be six processes all started by the same command.

Redirection of Input and Output _____

In both DOS and UNIX, you can redirect input from its usual source or output from its usual destination. Standard input in both systems is the keyboard; standard output is the screen. If you want input from another source or output to another destination, you have to use redirection. Since redirection was borrowed from UNIX, both operating systems use the same notation:

```
<        Redirect input
>        Redirect output
>>       Redirect output and append
```

You can think of these symbols as arrows pointing in the direction of the flow of processing.

Redirection of Input

Redirection of input allows you to prepare a file in advance and then allow a command to read the file. The **sort** command of either DOS or UNIX can read from a file through redirection. Another command that can read from a file in this way is the UNIX **mail** command. This command will be described in detail in the next chapter. For now, suppose you would like to send a message stored in file **new.time** via electronic mail to a user named Henry. So you begin by displaying the text:

```
$ cat new.time
Our meeting has been postponed
until next Monday at 10:00 AM.
Can you make it then?
$ _
```

The message is now in place in a file. To send it to user Henry, you can use redirection, as shown here:

```
$ mail henry < new.time
$ _
```

The redirection symbol (<) instructs the UNIX shell to take its input from file **new.time** instead of from the keyboard. The shell finds this file, reads its contents, and sends the message via electronic mail to user Henry.

Redirection of Output

Redirection of output allows you to send output of a command to a file instead of to the video screen, thereby giving you a permanent record instead of a fleeting glance. Earlier in this chapter, you tried four variations of the **ls** command to display a list of files in a directory. In each of those variations, the list appeared on the screen. By using redirection, you can send the file list to a file instead of the screen. Here is an example with the **ls** command:

```
$ ls -l > files
$ _
```

The output goes directly to a file called **files** and there is no screen display. To view the list afterward, you can use the **cat** command to display the contents of **files**, as illustrated here:

```
$ cat files
total 13
-rwxr-----  1  bill     6782  Feb  3  10:54  addendum
drwx--x---  1  bill      367  Mar 15  08:37  balance
-rw-r--r--  2  bill     9285  Apr 22  15:21  call-125
drwx------  1  bill      294  Jan 18  11:46  deadline
-rwxrw----  1  bill     8349  Dec 17  08:59  end.odd
-rw-r-----  1  bill        0  Dec 18  13:46  files
-rw-rw-rw-  5  bill     7956  May 24  10:03  first
$ _
```

Note that **files** includes itself in the list—before any information has been written to it. In DOS, redirection of output is generally to a hardware device. In UNIX, it is to a file. However, each hardware device is represented in a UNIX system as a file in directory /**dev**. So you can redirect output to a hardware device in UNIX as well as DOS.

If you want to collect a series of file lists in one file, you can use the redirection symbol for appending text (>>). For example, suppose you want to want to make lists for directories **past**, **present**, and **future** and store them all together in a file called **time.list**. These command lines show you how you could do this:

```
$ ls -l past >> time.list
$ ls -l present >> time.list
$ ls -l future >> time.list
$ _
```

The symbol for appending text (>>) is used in the above example so that the second and third lists will not overwrite file **time.list**. After you've executed the third **ls −l** command, **time.list** contains all three lists, one after the other. If you used the ordinary symbol (>) instead, **time.list** would contain only the third list; the first would be replaced by the second and the second would be replaced by the third.

If the target file (in this instance **time.list**) doesn't already exist, with either symbol (> or >>), the target file is created. If the target file does exist, the ordinary symbol (>) causes the file to be overwritten, while the appending symbol (>>) causes the new text to be appended to the existing text.

You can dispose of a UNIX file by redirecting it to a file in the /**dev** directory known as /**dev/null**. We'll defer examples to later chapters in the book.

Connecting Processes _____

If you want to process a file using two different commands consecutively, you can use redirection. Just redirect the output of the first command to a file; then redirect the input of the second command from the file you just created. But there's an easier way.

Using Pipes

Pipes are another feature that DOS has borrowed from UNIX. Pipes are one method for connecting processes that can make your work easier. With a pipe, the output of one process becomes the input of another, eliminating the need for temporary intermediate files.

You may have used pipes in DOS with commands like FIND and SORT, as in the following example:

```
C:\> DIR ¦ SORT
```

This feature works the same way in UNIX. For example, suppose you wanted to concatenate three files and send them to the printer as one file. You could use the **cat** (concatenate) command with a pipe to the **lp** (line printer) command, as shown in the following command line:

```
$ cat start middle finish ¦ lp
request id is nec-178 (1 file)
$ _
```

In the example just shown, you concatenate files **start**, **middle**, and **finish** to form one large file, which you pipe to the **lp** command for printing. As the system message indicates, the **lp** command recognizes only one file.

Using Tees

The UNIX **tee** command, which has no counterpart in DOS, allows you to have your cake and eat it too. With the **tee** command, which works in conjunction with a pipe, you can write output to a file and display it on the screen at the same time. You get the advantage of viewing output immediately and storing it for future reference all at once. In the example that follows, you display the names of the files in a directory and also store the list in a file names **file.list**:

```
$ ls -1 ¦ tee file.list
total 13
-rwxr-----  1  bill      6782  Feb  3  10:54  addendum
drwx--x---  1  bill       367  Mar 15  08:37  balance
-rw-r--r--  2  bill      9285  Apr 22  15:21  call-125
drwx------  1  bill       294  Jan 18  11:46  deadline
-rwxrw----  1  bill      8349  Dec 17  08:59  end.odd
-rw-rw-rw-  5  bill      7956  May 24  10:03  first
$ _
```

This command line, illustrated in Figure 4-1, gives you an immediate display and also a permanent record in a disk file.

Any time you want to take another look at the list, you can display it using the **cat** command:

```
$ cat file.list
total 13
-rwxr-----  1  bill      6782  Feb  3  10:54  addendum
drwx--x---  1  bill       367  Mar 15  08:37  balance
-rw-r--r--  2  bill      9285  Apr 22  15:21  call-125
drwx------  1  bill       294  Jan 18  11:46  deadline
-rwxrw----  1  bill      8349  Dec 17  08:59  end.odd
-rw-rw-rw-  5  bill      7956  May 24  10:03  first
$ _
```

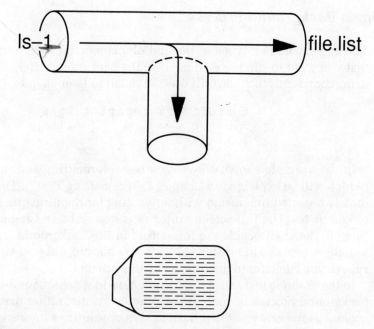

Figure 4-1. A Tee Illustrated

Background Processing

As mentioned earlier, *multitasking* is one of the main features of UNIX that really separates it from DOS. With multitasking, each user can have more than one process active in the system at any given moment. What makes multitasking possible is the concept of *foreground* processes and *background* processes. Foreground processes require user interaction from beginning to end and do not relinquish the screen. Background processes run unobtrusively and allow you to begin another process immediately.

For example, you could begin printing on a large file as a background process. Then you could immediately begin editing another file in the foreground. Printing would go on in the background, while you performed editing in the foreground. And this is only two processes. The UNIX system allows you to have five or six background processes running if necessary. **NOTE**: If too many users run too many processes simultaneously, system performance may suffer.

Running a Background Process

The ampersand (&), typed at the end of a command line, informs the shell that you want to run the command in the background. Here is an example, using commands that you will learn in detail in later chapters:

```
$ troff -cm report ¦ lp &
356
$ vi memo
```

In the example shown above, you begin formatting and printing **report** (which will be explained in Chapter 7, "Formatting Text"). Then you immediately begin editing **memo** without waiting for the formatting and printing to complete. (The full-screen editor **vi** is described in Chapter 6, "Editing Text.") The shell begins the formatting in the background, and the kernel assigns a process identifier (356). If you should have to stop formatting **report**, you can refer to the process by this number.

In the example just shown, you don't have to worry about the output of the background process (since it is going to the printer, rather than back to your screen). However, you often have to take precautions to prevent your background process from interfering with your foreground process. The way to do this is to redirect background output to a file. Otherwise, it will write over the screen while you are working with your foreground process.

Checking on Background Processes

After you've started a background process in a UNIX system, you can check on it to find out its present status. Has it completed? Is it still running? Or has it developed problems? The **ps** (process status) command displays a status line for each process that you have started. Here is an example:

```
$ ps
PID       TTY       TIME      COMMAND
385       03        0:01      -ps
367       03        0:03      vi memo
356       03        0:05      troff -cm report
298       03        0:34      -sh
$ _
```

The four columns displayed by the **ps** command are process identifier (PID), terminal number (TTY), execution time in minutes and seconds (TIME), and the name of the command (COMMAND). The display shows four processes, including the background process (356). Under the COMMAND column, you can see that the shell (-sh) and process status command (-ps) are included.

Terminating a Background Process

If you ever have to terminate a background process, you can use the **kill** command. The only argument you need is the process identifier, which is first displayed when you request a background process and again each time you run the **ps** command. Here is an example, using the formatting process referred to above:

```
$ kill 356
$ _
```

The problem with the **kill** command is that it doesn't tell you the outcome. The only way to find out whether or not you have actually terminated the process is to run **ps** again, as shown here:

```
$ ps
PID        TTY        TIME       COMMAND
401        03         0:01       -ps
367        03         0:15       vi memo
356        03         0:17       troff -cm report
298        03         0:46       -sh
$ _
```

In the display shown above, the **ps** command indicates that your background process (356) is still active. Any time this happens, you can use a stronger command to complete the termination. Run the **kill** command with the **−9** option, which indicates that **kill** cannot be ignored or caught by the target process. Here is an example:

```
$ kill -9 356
$ _
```

The **−9** option gets the job done, but it involves some risk. If you use it with either process 0 or your own shell (in this instance, process 298), you will automatically log yourself out.

## CHAPTER 5

UTILITY PROGRAMS

I n this chapter you will learn how to use a few of the most common utility
programs in the UNIX system. With these, you will be able to take care of
such things as handling text, printing, finding text and files, sorting, performing computations, and displaying calendars. Some of the programs described
in this chapter have DOS counterparts; some do not.

Handling Text

This section deals with methods for concatenating files, creating a small file,
and displaying large files on your screen.

Concatenating Files

In an earlier chapter, you learned how to display a small file on the screen
with the UNIX **cat** command. Now you will learn how to use this command
to concatenate files. In DOS, you would use the COPY command with a plus
sign (+) to perform this function. For example, to concatenate a pair of DOS
files called **PART.1** and **PART.2** and store the result in a third file called
TOTAL, you would use the DOS command line:

```
C:\> COPY PART.1 + PART.2 TOTAL
```

To do the same thing in UNIX, use the **cat** command with redirection of
output to the target file. For example, to concatenate UNIX files **part.1** and
part.2 and send the result to **total**, use the UNIX command line:

```
$ cat part.1 part.2 > total
$ _
```

After you've executed this command line, file **total** contains the combined text from files **part.1** and **part.2**.

Creating a Small File

You sometimes have to create a small file for the system. One example might be a batch file (DOS) or a shell script (UNIX). Since the file is small, you may not want to take the time to use a full-featured word processor or text editor. So you use something smaller and simpler. In DOS, you use the COPY command with CON (console, the video screen) and the name of the target file. Then you terminate the text with CTRL Z (press F6, then ENTER). Here is an example of creating a small DOS file in a file called **MESSAGE**:

```
C:\> COPY CON MESSAGE
Here is a short message
to demonstrate how to
create a small file.
CTRL Z
              1 File(s) copied
C:\> _
```

The way to accomplish the same thing in UNIX is to use the **cat** command with redirection to the target file. Then terminate the text with CTRL D. Here is an example of creating a small UNIX file in a file called **message**:

```
$ cat > message
Here is a short message
to demonstrate how to
create a small file.
CTRL D
$ _
```

Once you press CTRL D, the three lines of text are written to file **message**. Then, once the file has been created, you can display its contents with the same **cat** command (without redirection), as shown here:

```
$ cat message
Here is a short message
to demonstrate how to
create a small file.
$ _
```

(The corresponding DOS command to display text in a DOS file is TYPE.)

Displaying Large Files

If you try to display a large file in either operating system, you may find that there is too much text to fit on the screen. The text will begin racing off the top of the screen and you won't be able to read it. Then you won't want to use the ordinary command for displaying text: TYPE (DOS) or **cat** (UNIX). Instead, you need one of the following commands:

```
MORE (DOS)
pg (UNIX)
more (XENIX)
```

Each of these will display only enough text to fill one screen and then pause for your next response. For example, if you use the UNIX **pg** (page) command, one page will be displayed, along with a colon (:) at the bottom of the screen. Then you can press ENTER to display the next page, as illustrated below:

```
$ pg report
INTRODUCTION
This report describes the activities of the company for the
.
.
.
until the end of the quarter. Then sales will continue to
: _
```

The XENIX **more** command is similar to the UNIX **pg** command, but **more** offers a much wider choice of options at each pause. Here is an example of displaying a large file with **more**:

```
$ more report
INTRODUCTION
This report describes the activities of the company for the
.
.
.
until the end of the quarter. Then sales will continue to
--More-- (4%)
```

When the prompt appears at the bottom of the screen, you can proceed by selecting one of these options:

- Press ENTER to display one more line of text
- Press the space bar to display the next entire page

- Begin searching for text by typing a slash (/) and the desired text, as illustrated here:

/text

- Press ESC to terminate the **more** command and return to the shell prompt

Printing Text

One of the main reasons for entering text into a file is to print it on your printer. In this section, we'll discuss printing on the UNIX system, which is considerably more complex than printing on a DOS system.

There are several ways you can print text in DOS. One is to copy a file to **PRN**; another is to use the PRINT command. Here is an example of printing with the COPY command:

`C:\> COPY A:REPORT PRN`

To print text in UNIX, the command to use is **lp** (line printer). The main difference between UNIX and DOS is that you can have many printers attached to a single UNIX system, with one designated the default printer. The **lp** command is set up to route text to any printer in the UNIX system. To begin, assume that you want to print on the system's default printer. So you enter a command like

```
$ lp report
request id is lw-173 (1 file)
$ _
```

Because the UNIX system works with many users, your printing job probably won't be carried out immediately. Instead, the system will place your request in a queue and then perform actual printing when scheduling allows it. The **lp** command's response to your command line includes information about the queueing of your printing job. You will see a printer name (lw), a sequence number (173), and the number of files you are submitting. If you should have to cancel the printing job, you can use the identifier with a **cancel** command

```
$ cancel lw-173
$ _
```

The UNIX **lp** command, like the DOS PRINT command, allows you to queue more than one file at once

```
$ lp sec.1 sec.2 sec.3 sec.4 sec.5
request id is lw-189 (5 files)
$ _
```

The five files are queued for printing on the default printer under a common identifier. If you cancel this printing job, you remove all five files from the queue.

Options That Can Help You

When you place a printing job in the system queue, you may find that there are quite a few jobs ahead of yours. If those other printing jobs are very long, yours may be delayed for some time. Two **lp** options can make the delay a little more tolerable.

The − **m** (mail) options instructs **lp** to send you a message through the UNIX mail system as soon as your printing job is done. Enter the command line:

```
$ lp -m sec.6 sec.7 sec.8
request id is lw-195 (3 files)
$ _
```

The − **c** (copy) option instructs **lp** to make copies of your file(s) as a backup. If the system should lose track of your original(s), **lp** can use the backup(s) instead. Here is how you would enter the command line:

```
$ lp -c sec.9 sec.10
request id is lw-203 (2 files)
$ _
```

Requesting a Particular Printer

Until now, you have sent all printing jobs to the default printer (in these examples called **lw**). If your system has several printers, you can always send printing jobs to any printer that is working. Just include the − **d** (direct) option in your **lp** command line. For example, suppose one of the printers on your system is called epson_2. If you want a certain job printed on that printer, you can enter a command line that includes the − **d** option and names that printer, as shown here:

```
$ lp -depson_2 memo
request id is epson_2-108 (1 file)
$ _
```

The system response includes in its identifier the name of the printer that you requested. Your printing job is now queued for printer epson_2, rather than the default printer lw. Note that the name of the printer you are requesting is typed immediately after the **−d** without a space. Names for printers vary greatly from one system to another and may be completely different from the sample names used in this book. You can use only those names that have been specifically set up for your system.

Requesting a Particular Class

As you just learned in the previous subsection, the **lp** system allows you to request any printer attached to your UNIX system. But the **lp** system goes a step further. The various printers on your system can be grouped into *classes*, and you can direct your printing jobs to any class set up on your system. You do this by using the same **−d** option that you use for selecting a printer.

Printer classes are meant to group similar printers together. If your system has two dot-matrix printers, epson_1 and epson_2, it may not make any difference to you whether you print on one or the other. In fact, it may be more convenient for you to let the **lp** system choose the one that is least busy. If the dot matrix printers on your system belong to class *matrix*, then you can direct printing to one of them by using a command line like the following:

```
$ lp -dmatrix report
request id is epson_1-147 (1 file)
$ _
```

The system message uses the name of the printer that the system has selected for you (in this instance epson_1). You select the printer class; the **lp** system selects the actual printer. If your system is set up for printer classes, this is probably the best way to request printing.

The names for classes vary as much as the names for printers. Let's complete the above example with a full set of printers. Suppose the printers on your system belong to three classes: daisy-wheel printers, dot-matrix printers, and laser printers. Then suppose the three classes have the following

wheel	matrix	laser
diablo	epson_1	lw
nec_1	epson_2	ljet_1
nec_2		ljet_2
qume		

Figure 5-1. Three Printer Classes

names: **wheel**, **matrix**, and **laser**. All the classes and printers are portrayed in Figure 5-1.

According to Figure 5-1, this system has nine printers grouped into three classes. There are four daisy-wheel printers, two dot-matrix printers, and three laser printers. On this hypothetical system, you are free to select any of the three classes available: *wheel*, *matrix*, or *laser*.

Displaying the Queue

You can use the **lpstat** (printer status) command to determine the status of jobs that you have submitted for printing. (On some systems like Sun and NeXt, the command may be called **lpq**.) Here is an example of the **lpstat** command and its display:

```
$ lpstat
total 15
lw-189            bill        123405      Nov 9 10:57 on lw
lw-195            bill         89638      Nov 9 11:04
lw-203            bill         64712      Nov 9 11:11
epson_2-108       bill         10936      Nov 9 11:18
epson_1-147       bill         38903      Nov 9 11:26
$ _
```

The display shows five printing jobs in the queue, with one of them (lw-189) currently being completed on the printer. The information displayed above is stored in a directory called **/usr/spool/lpd**.

Finding Files _____

DOS has a FIND command, which is used to find text in a file. UNIX has a **find** command, which is used to find files in directories. The DOS FIND command is actually more like the UNIX **grep** command, which is discussed in the next section. With all this confusion out of the way, let's consider the UNIX **find** command, which has no counterpart in DOS.

With the UNIX **find** command, you can search for files and take action. A common use of **find** is to search for files and display their names on the screen. But you can also back them up or apply any other suitable UNIX command to them, such as the one for copying, moving, or deleting files. The search can be based on filename, type of file, owner, group, permissions, or date of last modification. These search criteria give you a wide variety of ways to pinpoint a particular file. See Figure 5-2 for a general command line for the **find** command.

The command line begins, of course, with the **find** command. Next, you have to specify the names of any directory (or directories) in which you

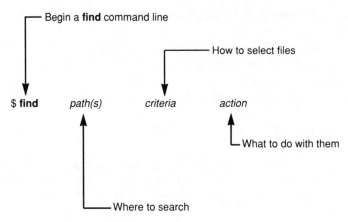

Figure 5-2. General Command Line for find

would like to direct the search. Then you give the search criteria, followed by a description of what to do with any files that are selected.

Before taking any action that may alter your files, it's a good idea to begin with an exploratory **find** command line that merely displays the names of the files you are looking for. For example, here's a command line to locate all files in directory **/usr** (or any of its subdirectories) that are named **help**. Use the **-name** option to search by filename and the **-print** option to display the names on your screen. (Remember, *print* doesn't really mean print in UNIX.) Here is how the command line and its output might look:

```
$ find /usr -name help -print
/usr/alice/admin/help
/usr/bill/test/help
/usr/cynthia/memos/old/help
/usr/dennis/letters/help
/usr/edy/FUTURE/help
$ _
```

The output in the example is five filenames displayed under the command line. These five names represent all the files in directory **/usr** that are named **help**. (As long as they are in different directories, files can share the same name.) Here is a more detailed look at the command line shown above (see Figure 5-3).

Referring to Figure 5-3, the first two items on the command line (**find** and **/usr**) are self-explanatory. Each command line must begin with the **find** command and the name of a directory (or names of directories) to search. So we'll

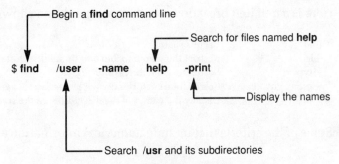

Figure 5-3. Command Line for Finding Files

describe the two remaining items on the command line (search criteria and action).

Search Criteria

Search criteria may include a name (as in the example shown above), a file type, or numerical information. Some of the criteria that include names and file types are shown in Table 5-1.

Table 5-1. Search Criteria with Names and Types

Criterion	Description
−type f	Search for an ordinary file
−type d	Search for a directory
−name *file*	Search for a file (or files) named *file*
−newer *file*	Search for files modified more recently than a file named *file*
−user *name*	Search for files owned by user *name*
−group *name*	Search for files owned by members of group *name*

The following example illustrates some of the search criteria described in Table 5-1. In this example, you are searching directory **/bin** for a subdirectory owned by a member of group **coyote**:

```
$ find /bin -type d -group coyote -print
/bin/time
/bin/place
$ _
```

Here is a detailed breakdown of the command line shown above:

find	Begin a search
/bin	Restrict the search to **/bin** and its subdirectories
−type d	Search for directories only
−group coyote	Search for directories owned by members of group **coyote**
−print	Display the names of the directories on the screen

Some of the criteria that include numerical information are shown in Table 5-2.

Table 5-2. Search Criteria with Numerical Information

Criterion	Description
−size +b	Search for files larger than b blocks
−size b	Search for files with exactly b blocks
−size −b	Search for files smaller than b blocks
−links +n	Search for files with more than n links
−links n	Search for files with exactly n links
−links −n	Search for files with fewer than n links
−atime +d	Search for files accessed more than d days
−atime d	Search for files accessed exactly d days
−atime −d	Search for files accessed fewer than d days
−ctime +d	Search for files changed more than d days
−ctime d	Search for files changed exactly d days
−ctime −d	Search for files changed fewer than d days
−mtime +d	Search for files modified more than d days
−mtime d	Search for files modified exactly d days
−mtime −d	Search for files modified fewer than d days

The following example illustrates some of the search criteria described in Table 5-2. In this example, you are searching directory **/usr** for all files that are larger than 5 blocks and that were changed exactly 30 days ago:

```
$ find /usr -size 5 -ctime 30 -print
/usr/charles/memos/memo.125
/usr/dana/admin/dept.ltr
/usr/henry/test/project.142
$ _
```

Here is a detailed breakdown of the command line shown above:

find	Begin a search
/usr	Restrict the search to **/usr** and its subdirectories
−size 5	Search for files larger than 5 blocks
−ctime 30	Search for files that were changed exactly 30 days ago
−print	Display the names of the directories on the screen

In UNIX System V, one block is 1,024 bytes. Blocks are used in UNIX to measure larger amounts of text and data.

Action Statements

In the examples used so far in this chapter, you have seen only the **−print** statement. Table 5-3 lists action statements that you can use with the **find** command. Some of them refer to the **cpio** command, a backup command that is described in Chapter 13, "Managing Disks and Tapes."

Table 5-3. Action Statements

Statement	Description
−print	Display the full pathname of each file matched
−exec *command*	Execute *command* unconditionally with each file matched
−ok *command*	Execute *command* with interactive confirmation with each file matched
−cpio *device*	Copy each file matched to *device* in **cpio** format
−depth	Used only before **-exec cpio** or **-ok cpio**, copy all files in a directory and then the directory itself

Here is a note about the **−exec** and **−ok** statements, which are used to run UNIX commands. If the UNIX command requires a filename (or filenames) for an argument, you must type { } \; after the name of the command (in the space where the argument would ordinarily appear). The pair of empty braces ({ }) holds a place for the name of each file matched during the search, using that filename as an argument for the command. See the example that follows for an illustration.

The following example shows you how to perform a common administrative task for a UNIX system: removing **core** files. Without going into details, these are pesky files that can clutter up your system if you leave them lying around. (A **core** file can also be handy if used right after a system failure.) In this example, you are searching for all files named **core** throughout the system that are more than five days old and removing them.

```
$ find / -name core -atime +5 -ok rm {} \;
< rm ... /usr/ben/letters/core > ? y
< rm ... /usr/dale/memos/core > ? y
< rm ... /usr/ellen/type/core > ? y
 .
 .
 .
$ _
```

Here is a detailed breakdown of the previous command line:

find	Begin a search
/	Search all directories in the system
−name core	Search for files named **core**
−atime +5	Search for files that were accessed more than five days ago
−ok rm { } \;	Remove all files matched (with confirmation)

In the output of this command line you will see the name of each matched file displayed with a question mark following. You can enter either **y** (yes) or **n** (no) to confirm the deletion. Yes means "carry out the deletion"; no means "don't delete the file."

Searching For Text

Searching One File

The DOS FIND shares a common name with the UNIX **find** command. But in its function the DOS FIND command corresponds to the UNIX **grep** command. The **grep** command is for searching for text in a file (or in several files). To demonstrate its use, we'll use the short file named **message** that you entered near the beginning of this chapter:

```
Here is a short message
to demonstrate how to
create a small file.
```

Suppose you wanted to search this file for the line that contains the word *small*. In DOS, you would use a command line like this:

```
C:\> FIND "small" A:MESSAGE
----------a:message
create a small file.
C:\> _
```

In UNIX, you would use a command line like this:

```
$ grep small message
create a small file.
$ _
```

As the two preceding examples show, the DOS FIND command and the UNIX **grep** command are quite similar. However, the UNIX **grep** command has a few more features (and also a strange name).

To demonstrate additional similarity between the two commands, suppose you want to recall the name of a file in the current directory that includes the letters **call**. In DOS, you would use a command like this:

```
C:\> DIR ¦ FIND "CALL"
call-125   9285 Apr 22 15:21
C:\> _
```

In UNIX, you would use a command line like this:

```
$ ls -l ¦ grep call
-rw-r--r--  2  bill       9285  Apr 22  15:21  call-125
$ _
```

This time, neither FIND nor **grep** required a filename because the text (a directory listing) came through a pipe.

Searching Several Files

The DOS FIND command and the UNIX **grep** command both allow you to search several files at the same time. We'll demonstrate the UNIX **grep** command with a few sample files. Suppose your company has a bowling league, with contestants from different wings (east, west, and south). To keep the examples simple, we'll restrict the number of bowlers to four from each wing. If you have each time stored in a different file, the three files could look like this:

```
$ cat bowl.west
Henley, Bob             1004        263.1
Thomas, Jane            0839        244.8
Albert, Ned             0967        241.2
Brown, Laura            1107        236.7

$ cat bowl.east
Peters, Alice           1026        258.3
Henley, Bill            0792        253.5
Jeffreys, Paul          0948        247.0
Vicente, Nancy          1243        239.4
```

```
$ cat bowl.south
Lawrence, Pete          0651        268.6
Jeffreys, Clara         0885        252.9
Thomas, Ted             1019        243.2
Lao, Nina               1270        238.5
```

Any set of files can be used, but files with information organized into columns make it a little easier to demonstrate the features of **grep** and **sort**. In the files shown above, you see a name on the left, an employee number in the middle, and a bowling score on the right. The items are separated by tabs, but they could also be separated by blank spaces. We'll use **grep** to help answer a few questions:

1. Does an Albert play for the west wing?
   a. Check file **bowl.west** for **Albert**:

   ```
   $ grep Albert bowl.west
   Albert, Ned             0967        241.2
   $ _
   ```

   b. Answer: Yes, Ned Albert.

2. Does a Thomas play for the east wing?
   a. Check file **bowl.east** for **Thomas**:

   ```
   $ grep Thomas bowl.east
   $ _
   ```

   b. Answer: No (there is no output).

3. Does Clara Jeffreys play for the south wing?
   a. Check file **bowl.south** for **Jeffreys, Clara**:

   ```
   $ grep "Jeffreys, Clara" bowl.south
   Jeffreys, Clara         0885        252.9
   $ _
   ```

   b. Answer: Yes.

The quotation marks around "Jeffreys, Clara" were required because you have two words separated by a blank space.

4. Which teams do the Henleys play for?
   a. Check all three files for **Henley**:

```
$ grep Henley bowl.*
bowl.west:Henley, Bob              1004        263.1
bolw.east:Henley, Bill             0792        253.5
```

b. Answer: east and west wings.

You can use the wildcard symbol (*) to search all three files (**bowl.west**, **bowl.east**, and **bowl.south**) with the same **grep** command. As the previous example shows, when you search more than one file, **grep** inserts a filename in front of each line of output.

Using Regular Expressions

The **grep** command line allows wildcards and a variety of *metacharacters* in searches. When you use these characters in searches, you form *regular expressions*. For example, to search for either **Bill** or **bill**, you could use the following expression:

```
[Bb]ill
```

When you use this notation, **grep** searches for either of the characters between brackets (B or b). Here is a list of metacharacters you can use in regular expressions:

^	Beginning of line
.	Any one character
[ ]	Characters enclosed
$	End of line
*	Any number of characters
\	Escape character

To search for any of the above characters in a file, precede it with the escape character (\ ). For example, to search for a period, type \. in the search string.

You can use regular expressions in many different ways. In the examples that follow, however, we'll concentrate on those that relate to numerical expressions. Again, we'll use **grep** to help us answer questions.

1. Did anyone average exactly 247 points?
   a. Check all files for **247\.0**:

```
$ grep 247\.0 bowl.*
bowl.east:Jeffreys, Paul           0948        247.0
$ _
```

b. Answer: Yes (Paul Jeffreys).

2. Did anyone average higher than 260 (up to 299.9)?
   a. Check all files for numbers larger than 260:

```
$ grep "2[6-9][0-9]\.[0-9]" bowl.*
bowl.west:Henley, Bob          1004      263.1
bowl.south:Lawrence, Pete      0651      268.6
$ _
```

b. Answer: Yes, two players.

The numeric searches just shown illustrate the use of the escape character (\) to include the decimal point. Without the backslash, **grep** would read the period as a metacharacter. (Another thing to note is that the fields aren't aligned in the output display.)

Comparing FIND and grep

As mentioned earlier, the UNIX **grep** command shares some features with the DOS FIND command. To begin with, the two commands follow similar rules of syntax:

```
C\> FIND [option(s)] "string" filename(s)
$ grep [option(s)] "string" filename(s)
```

With FIND, the quotation marks around the search string are always required; with **grep**, they are required only if the search string includes a regular expression or more than one word. If you want to search more than one file with FIND, you have to give each name explicitly; with **grep**, you can use

Table 5-4. FIND and grep Options

FIND	grep	Function
	−b	Display a block number in front of each line matched.
/C	−c	Count the number of matched lines but not the lines themselves.
	−i	Ignore case while searching.
	−l	Display filename(s) but not lines of text.
/N	−n	Display line numbers with text.
	−s	Suppress file error messages during the search.
/V	−v	Invert the search (match only lines that do **not** contain the search string).

wildcard characters to identify a group of files. A comparison of major options is given in Table 5-4.

Finally, the UNIX **grep** command is accompanied by two related search commands, **fgrep** (fast **grep**) and **egrep** (extended **grep**). The **fgrep** command accepts only literal strings; the **grep** command also accepts regular expressions; the **egrep** command accepts compound expressions.

Sorting

The UNIX **sort** command corresponds to the DOS SORT command. The two commands have many things in common. Both, in their basic forms, sort lines in ascending order (from A to Z, or from 0 to 9), starting with the character in the first column. For example:

```
$ cat trees
birch
aspen
redwood
pine
ash
fir
$ _
```

If you enter the **sort** command without any options, the lines will be alphabetized:

```
$ sort trees
ash
aspen
birch
fir
pine
redwood
$ _
```

When you use the DOS SORT command, you have to redirect input from the input file. With the UNIX **sort** command, redirection is unnecessary; you just name the input file at the end of the command line.

Selecting Fields

With both the DOS and UNIX commands, the default is to begin sorting at the first column. The DOS SORT command allows you to begin the sort in another *column*, using the / + c notation. The UNIX **sort** command allows you to begin the sort at the beginning of another *field*. For an example of fields, take another look at one of the bowling files from the previous section:

```
$ cat bowl.west
Henley, Bob                1004          263.1
Thomas, Jane               0839          244.8
Albert, Ned                0967          241.2
Brown, Laura               1107          236.7
$ _
```

As viewed by the **sort** command, each open space in **bowl.west** (blank space or tab) represents a *field separator*, meaning that each line in the file contains four *fields*: last name, first name, employee number, and bowling average. You can display this file as shown in Figure 5-4.

Last name	First name	Employee no.	Average
Henley,	Bob	1004	263.1
Thomas,	Jane	0839	244.8
Albert,	Ned	0967	241.2
Brown,	Laura	1107	236.7
Field 1	**Field 2**	**Field 3**	**Field 4**

Figure 5-4. The Fields in a Bowling File

If you want to sort a file like this by employee number with the DOS SORT command, you have to begin by figuring out the column in which employee number begins. With the UNIX **sort** command, all you have to know is that employee number is the third field. Then use **+2** (skip the first two fields) in the command line, as shown here:

```
$ sort +2 bowl.west
Thomas, Jane               0839          244.8
Albert, Ned                0967          241.2
Henley, Bob                1004          263.1
Brown, Laura               1107          236.7
$ _
```

In the preceding example, the fourth field (bowling average) is included in the sort, even though it doesn't make any difference. If you want to **exclude** the fourth field, include **−3** (stop sorting after the third field):

```
$ sort +2 -3 bowl.west
Thomas, Jane               0839          244.8
Albert, Ned                0967          241.2
Henley, Bob                1004          263.1
Brown, Laura               1107          236.7
$ _
```

The outcome is the same for the two examples just shown. However, the notation **+2 −3** means, "Start sorting after field 2; stop after field 3" (in other words, "Sort only field 3"). This is illustrated below:

```
Start sorting                                    Stop sorting
after field 2                                    after field 3

Thomas,        Jane       │ 0839     │ 244.8
Albert,        Ned        │ 0967     │ 241.2
Henley,        Bob        │ 1004     │ 263.1
Brown,         Laura      │ 1107     │ 236.7

Field 1        Field 2    │ Field 3  │ Field 4
```

Using Sort Options

The DOS SORT command has only one additional option; the UNIX **sort** command has many more options (see Table 5-5).

Table 5-5. Options for the sort Command

SORT	sort	Function
	−b	Ignore leading blanks when sorting.
	−d	Sort in dictionary order.
	−f	Fold uppercase letters onto lowercase (CASE, Case, and case are identical).
	−i	Ignore non-printing characters.
	−n	Sort a field as numeric, allowing blanks, minus signs, zeroes, or decimal points if necessary (option −b automatically)
	−M	Sort months (JAN, FEB, MAR, ..., DEC).
	−o file	Store output in file—same as > **file**
/R	−r	Sort in reverse order (Z to A or 9 to 0).
	−t x	Make x the field separator.
	−u	Sort uniquely (discard extra lines if identical).
	−y k	Reserve k kilobytes for this sort.
	−z n	Allow a maximum of n characters per input line.

You can use two of these options to sort the lines by bowling average (field 4). In the following example, options **−n** (numeric) and **−r** (reverse order) will be bundled (that is, combined into a single expression, **−nr**).

```
$ sort -nr +3 bowl.west
Henley, Bob              1004        263.1
Thomas, Jane             0839        244.8
Albert, Ned              0967        241.2
Brown, Laura             1107        236.7
$ _
```

Sorting More Than One File

In the previous example, the order isn't changed by sorting. So we'll enter another command line that is nearly the same. But this time we'll sort all three files:

```
$ sort -nr +3 bowl.*
Lawrence, Pete          0651        268.6
Henley, Bob             1004        263.1
Peters, Alice           1026        258.3
Henley, Bill            0792        253.5
Jeffreys, Clara         0885        252.9
Jeffreys, Paul          0948        247.0
Thomas, Jane            0839        244.8
Thomas, Ted             1019        243.2
Albert, Ned             0967        241.2
Vicente, Nancy          1243        239.4
Lao, Nina               1270        238.5
Brown, Laura            1107        236.7
$ _
```

In the previous example, you can use the **sort** command to merge and sort several files simultaneously. The list shown above includes all lines from all three files, sorted in reverse order by bowling average.

Sending the Output to a File

We'll conclude this section on sorting with a discussion of sending the output of a sort to a file. You can accomplish this by using redirection to the file. Here is an example:

1. Sort the input file and send the output to file **emplno.west**:

```
$ sort +2 bowl.west > emplno.west
$ _
```

2. Display the output file:

```
$ cat emplno.west
Thomas, Jane            0839        244.8
Albert, Ned             0967        241.2
Henley, Bob             1004        263.1
Brown, Laura            1107        236.7
$ _
```

You can also sort multiple files and send the output to another file. Here is an example:

1. Sort all three files and send the output to file **bowl.avg**:

```
$ sort -nr +3 bowl.* > bowl.avg
$ _
```

2. Display the output file:

```
$ cat bowl.avg
Lawrence, Pete          0651        268.6
Henley, Bob             1004        263.1
Peters, Alice           1026        258.3
Henley, Bill            0792        253.5
Jeffreys, Clara         0885        252.9
Jeffreys, Paul          0948        247.0
Thomas, Jane            0839        244.8
Thomas, Ted             1019        243.2
Albert, Ned             0967        241.2
Vicente, Nancy          1243        239.4
Lao, Nina               1270        238.5
Brown, Laura            1107        236.7
$ _
```

Other Programs

In this section we'll discuss three UNIX programs that have no counterparts in DOS. Each of the first two converts your terminal into a calculator; the third is useful for creating calendars.

Using the Desk Calculator

The **dc** command turns your terminal into a simple, elementary desk calculator. The program is easy to use, as illustrated by the following sample session:

```
$ dc            Begin a session
9               ENTER 9
4               ENTER 4
+               Add the two numbers entered
p               Print (that is, display) the sum 13
2+p             Add 2 and display the new sum 15
12*p            Multiply by 12 and display the product 180
9/p             Divide by 9 and display the quotient 20
12-p            Subtract 12 and display the difference 8
q               Quit (end the session with dc)
$ _
```

Use the **dc** command to begin a session and the **q** instruction to end a session. The command includes a number of other features, such as number bases, scaling, subscripts, functions, and logical control. Some of these features will be described in the subsection that follows.

Using the High-Precision Calculator

The **bc** command gives you a much more sophisticated and versatile calculator with high precision, variables, and up to 99 digits after the decimal point. The following sample session shows what is possible with the **bc** command:

```
$ bc                    Begin a session
13 + 17                 Add two numbers and display the sum
30 12 - 21              Subtract one number from another
-9 9 * 8                Multiply two numbers together
72 48 / 3               Divide one number by another
16 sqrt(49)             Take the square root of a number
7 scale = 6             Request six digits after the decimal point
s = sqrt(29)            Assign a value to variable s
s                       Display the value of s (to six places)
5.385165
define f(a,b) {         Define function f
  auto c                   with automatic variable c
  c = a + b                that accepts the sum of a and b
  return(c)                and returns the sum as the value of f
}                       End of function f
x = sqrt(29)            Assign to variable x the square root of 29
y = sqrt(17)            Assign to variable y the  square root of 17
f(x,y)                  Use function f to compute the sum of x and y
9.508270
quit                    Quit (end the session with bc)
$ _
```

The **bc** calculator supports a number of other features, such as comments, arrays, and conversion of numbers from one base to another. For additional features, you can include the −**l** (library) option, which supports exponential (**e**), natural logarithm (**l**), sine (**s**), arctangent (**a**), and Bessel (**j(n,x)**) functions. To include this mathematical library, enter the command line as follows:

$$\text{\$ bc -l}$$

Finally, you can store complex functions in a separate file and then retrieve the file when you begin a session with **bc**. For example, suppose you have stored the following factorial function in a file called **fact.bc**:

```
$ cat fact.bc
define f(n) {
   auto i,j
   j = 1
```

```
    for (i=1;i<=n;i++) j = j * i
    return (j)
}
$ _
```

By starting a session with the following command line, you can make the
function available during the session:

$$\text{\$ \textbf{bc fact.bc}}$$

The factorial function becomes available, and you can use it as many times
as necessary without having to retype it during your session with **bc**.

Displaying a Calendar

Another kind of calculator, the **cal** (calendar) command, allows you to display a calendar for any year from 1 A.D. to 9999 A.D. Here's an example for
displaying the calendar for 1066, the year of the Norman conquest of Eng-
land:

```
$ cal 1066

                         1066


              Jan                    Feb                    Mar
     S  M Tu  W Th  F  S     S  M Tu  W Th  F  S     S  M Tu  W Th  F  S
     1  2  3  4  5  6  7              1  2  3  4              1  2  3  4
     8  9 10 11 12 13 14     5  6  7  8  9 10 11     5  6  7  8  9 10 11
    15 16 17 18 19 20 21    12 13 14 15 16 17 18    12 13 14 15 16 17 18
    22 23 24 25 26 27 28    19 20 21 22 23 24 25    19 20 21 22 23 24 25
    29 30 31               26 27 28               26 27 28 29 30 31


              Apr                    May                    Jun
     S  M Tu  W Th  F  S     S  M Tu  W Th  F  S     S  M Tu  W Th  F  S
                    1        1  2  3  4  5  6              1  2  3
     2  3  4  5  6  7  8     7  8  9 10 11 12 13     4  5  6  7  8  9 10
     9 10 11 12 13 14 15    14 15 16 17 18 19 20    11 12 13 14 15 16 17
    16 17 18 19 20 21 22    21 22 23 24 25 26 27    18 19 20 21 22 23 24
    23 24 25 26 27 28 29    28 29 30 31            25 26 27 28 29 30
    30


              Jul                    Aug                    Sep
     S  M Tu  W Th  F  S     S  M Tu  W Th  F  S     S  M Tu  W Th  F  S
                    1        1  2  3  4  5              1  2
     2  3  4  5  6  7  8     6  7  8  9 10 11 12     3  4  5  6  7  8  9
     9 10 11 12 13 14 15    13 14 15 16 17 18 19    10 11 12 13 14 15 16
    16 17 18 19 20 21 22    20 21 22 23 24 25 26    17 18 19 20 21 22 23
    23 24 25 26 27 28 29    27 28 29 30 31         24 25 26 27 28 29 30
    30 31
```

```
        Oct                      Nov                      Dec
 S  M Tu  W Th  F  S      S  M Tu  W Th  F  S      S  M Tu  W Th  F  S
 1  2  3  4  5  6  7               1  2  3  4                     1  2
 8  9 10 11 12 13 14      5  6  7  8  9 10 11      3  4  5  6  7  8  9
15 16 17 18 19 20 21     12 13 14 15 16 17 18     10 11 12 13 14 15 16
22 23 24 25 26 27 28     19 20 21 22 23 24 25     17 18 19 20 21 22 23
29 30 31                 26 27 28 29 30           24 25 26 27 28 29 30
                                                  31
```

By entering a number from 1 to 12 just before the year, you can also display the calendar for a single month. For example, suppose you're interested in finding out the day of the week on which the Battle of Hastings took place. You can display the calendar for October 1066:

```
$ cal 10 1066
   October 1066
 S  M Tu  W Th  F  S
 1  2  3  4  5  6  7
 8  9 10 11 12 13 14
15 16 17 18 19 20 21
22 23 24 25 26 27 28
29 30 31
```

Answer: October 14 falls on a Saturday.

CHAPTER 6

EDITING TEXT

Because so many word-processing programs are available in the DOS world, few DOS users probably pay much attention to the **EDLIN** program. If you have WordPerfect or Word, then you probably use it for nearly all your memos, letters, and reports. The only time you would even consider using DOS's crude **EDLIN** program would be when you were setting up your machine and you needed to enter a system initialization file. Even then, there's a good chance you would use the **COPY** command instead of **EDLIN**.

For those who've never even heard of it, **EDLIN** is an awkward line editor that comes with DOS. This means that each line of text has a line number, and you have to use line numbers when you make editing changes. UNIX also has a program like this called **ed**. At one time, **ed** was the only UNIX program available for entering and editing text. However, in the 1970s, a program called **vi** (visual interpreter) was developed at the University of California. By the late 1980s, **vi** has almost completely replaced **ed** as a text-editing tool on UNIX systems.

Although the UNIX **ed** program is more similar to the DOS **EDLIN** program, we'll bypass both of them in this book and concentrate on **vi**. As a full-screen editor, **vi** at least comes close to approximating the sophistication and power that computer users are accustomed to today. To the best of my knowledge, few DOS users use **EDLIN** and few UNIX users still use **ed**.

To be precise, **vi** is the visual mode of another UNIX program called **ex**, which is an extended and enhanced version of **ed**. However, **vi** has overshadowed its parent program and taken on a life of its own. We'll refer to **ex** commands from time to time in this chapter. However, you will do most of your editing with **vi**.

Beginning and Ending a Session

To get started, you will learn how to start the **vi** editor, enter text, repeat and undo keystrokes, save your text, and return to the UNIX shell prompt. Before you can begin, you have to make sure your terminal has been identified to the UNIX. But since this isn't discussed until Chapter 14, "Managing Terminals," we won't go into this in any detail here.

A Complete Session

Now you will go through a complete session with **vi** from beginning to end. First, select an appropriate subdirectory to work in. With **vi**, you can name your file either at the beginning or end of an editing session. In the following session, we'll name it at the beginning of the session.

1. Start the editor:
   a. Enter the **vi** command, followed by a filename:

   ```
   $ vi sample.doc
   ```

   b. Soon you will see something like the following screen:

   ```
   ~
   ~
   ~
   ~
   ~
   ~
   ~
   ~
   ~
   ~
   ~
   "sample.doc" [New file]
   ```

2. Change to text entry mode:
   a. Press **a**, but not ENTER, to allow you to *append* text.
   b. Neither **a** nor any message will appear on the screen, but you are now free to enter text.

   ```
   One of vi's most vexing problems is that it doesn't
   show you clearly which mode you're in.
   ```

3. Enter new text:

a. Type the following, including ENTER at the end of each line and two spaces following each period:

```
The primary text editor for UNIX is vi  ENTER
-pronounced vee-eye.  Actually, vi is  ENTER
nothing more than the visual interpreter  ENTER
of the ex editor.  When you use vi, you  ENTER
are really using the ex editor.  ENTER
```

b. The text will appear on the screen as you type it, replacing tildes on the left line by line.

4. End text entry mode and return to **vi** command mode:
a. Press ESC (the escape key).
b. Nothing will appear on the screen, but you will go back to **vi** command mode.

5. Save the text in a file and end the session:
a. Type **:w** and press ENTER to save the text in file **sample.doc**.
b. First **:w** will appear at the bottom of the screen; then the following message:

```
"sample.doc" [New file] 5 lines, 186 characters
```

c. Type **:q** and press ENTER to leave **vi** and return to the shell prompt:

```
$ _
```

Review of the Session

You have just completed an entire editing session with **vi** and created a small document. Now we'll review the steps briefly:

1. You started **vi** by entering the **vi** command from the shell prompt.
2. You requested text entry mode by pressing **a** (append mode).
3. You entered text in text entry mode.
4. You returned to **vi** command mode. This mode is used for entering **vi** commands.
5. You saved the text by pressing **:w** and ended the session by pressing **:q**.

The write (**:w**) and quit (**:q**) commands you used in Step 5 were **ex** commands. Every **ex** command begins with a colon (:); the colon starts **ex** com-

Figure 6-1. Cursor Motion Keys

mand mode. You can enter the write and quitcommands separately, as you did above in Step 5, or you can enter them as a single command (**:wq**).

Cursor and Screen Motion

Whenever you use a text editor, you have to move the cursor from one location to another many times. Most of **vi**'s editing functions depend on the position and motion of the cursor.

Moving One Position

If your keyboard includes a set of arrow keys for cursor motion, as shown on the left in Figure 6-1, you can move the cursor with these keys. If not, you can use either of the alternative sets of cursor motion keys, as shown in the middle and on the right of Figure 6-1.

Since these are **vi** commands, you can use them only when you are in **vi** command mode. If you aren't sure which mode you're in, press ESC. A beep means you're in **vi** command mode.

Begin another session with the document you created earlier in this chapter to experiment with these cursor motion keys. Choose the set that you feel most comfortable with. This is the command for starting another session:

```
$ vi sample.doc
```

After trying out the cursor motion keys, add these two paragraphs to the document:

```
ENTER
Each time you start vi, you begin the    ENTER
program in vi command mode.  To enter    ENTER
text, press a (or one of the other    ENTER
letters) to change to text entry mode.    ENTER
Then press ESC to go back to vi command    ENTER
mode.
ENTER
```

```
To save your text, type :w and press   ENTER
Enter to write it to a file.  To end    ENTER
the editing session, type :q and press  ENTER
Enter.  Each colon (:) takes you into   ENTER
ex command mode; each Enter takes you    ENTER
back to vi command mode.  ENTER
```

After you've typed the two paragraphs, press ESC to go back to **vi** command mode; then type **:w** and press ENTER to save the text in **sample.doc**. A message like this will be displayed at the bottom of the screen:

```
"sample.doc" 20 lines, 596 characters
```

Repeating and Undoing

In a moment, we'll resume our discussion of cursor motion. But for now, here's a brief experiment to try repeating and undoing keystrokes:

1. Enter some additional text:
   a. With the cursor still on the last line of **sample.doc**, type

   ```
   ENTER
   Here are two extra lines to show how   ENTER
   you can repeat and undo keystrokes.  ENTER
   ESC
   ```

   b. You will see these two lines near the bottom of the screen.

2. Repeat what you just typed:
   a. Press period (.) but not ENTER.
   b. The bottom of the screen should look like this:

   ```
   Here are two extra lines to show how
   you can repeat and undo keystrokes.

   Here are two extra lines to show how
   you can repeat and undo keystrokes.
   _
   ~
   ~
   ```

3. Undo step 2:
   a. Press **u**, but not ENTER.
   b. The bottom of the screen will look like this again:

   ```
   Here are two extra lines to show how
   you can repeat and undo keystrokes.
   _
   ~
   ~
   ```

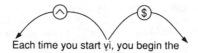

Each time you start vi, you begin the

Figure 6-2. Moving the Cursor to Either End of a Line

    a. Press **u** again to restore the copy.
    b. Press **u** once more to return to one paragraph.

4. Abandon all changes:
    a. Type **:q!** and press ENTER to leave **vi** without saving.
    b. The two extra lines will be gone, and you will return to the shell prompt:

      $ _

With the repeat command (.), you can duplicate a complex set of keystrokes. With the undo command (**u**), you can reverse the most recent change to your text—usually a deletion. When you undo a second time, you return your text to its original state. These two commands can be very handy whenever you use **vi**. Now we'll return to the subject of moving the cursor.

Moving to the End of the Line

You may recall using the metacharacters for searching at the beginning of a line (^) or the end of a line ($). These are the same keys you use in **vi** to move the cursor to the beginning of the current line (^) or the end of the line($). The results of these keys are illustrated in Figure 6-2.

Suppose the cursor is resting on the **v** in **vi**, as shown in Figure 6-2. If you press ^, the cursor will jump to the left end of the line. If you press **$**, it will jump to the right end.

Moving the Cursor by Words

You can use **w** to move the cursor to the first letter of the next word or **b** to move back to the first letter of the previous word, as shown in Figure 6-3. The **W** and **B** keys are nearly the same as **w** and **b**, except that **W** and **B** ignore punctuation, such as apostrophes ('). To **w** and **b**, a word like don't appears to be two words. To **W** and **B**, *don't* is a single word. When in doubt, use **W** and **B**. You can remember these keys by their mnemonic values:

Back: B   b
Word: W w

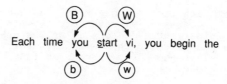

Figure 6-3. Moving the Cursor One Word

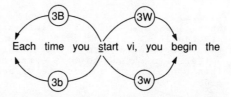

Figure 6-4. Moving the Cursor Several Words at Once

If the cursor is currently resting on the **s** in **start**, as shown in Figure 6-3, you can press **B** (or **b**) to move back one word and **W** (or **w**) to move forward one word. If you want to move several words at a time, you can include a *multiplier*. For example, to move the cursor three words at a time, you can use **3B** or **3W**, as shown in Figure 6-4.

Multipliers are very common in **vi** and can be included in a great variety of **vi** commands. In most instances, you can type the multiplier either before or after the command (**3W** or **W3**). However, for the sake of simplicity, we'll use multipliers in front of commands in this book.

Moving the Cursor by Sentences and Paragraphs

Once you're familiar with moving the cursor by words, the cursor commands for moving by sentences and paragraphs are easy to grasp. For sentences, each of which is assumed to end with a period and two blank spaces, use parentheses, as shown in Figure 6-5. Use a left parenthesis to move to the left (to the beginning of the previous sentence); use a right parenthesis to move to the right (to the beginning of the next sentence).

Suppose the cursor is resting on the **T** of **To enter** (the beginning of the second sentence). You can press **(** to move the cursor back to the beginning of the previous sentence or **)** to move to the beginning of the next sentence. Once again, to move more than one sentence at a time, you can include a multiplier. For example, to move three sentences at a time, you can use **3(** or **3)**.

If the cursor is currently resting somewhere in the middle of a sentence, **(** will move it to the beginning of the sentence, and **)** will move it to the beginning of the following sentence.

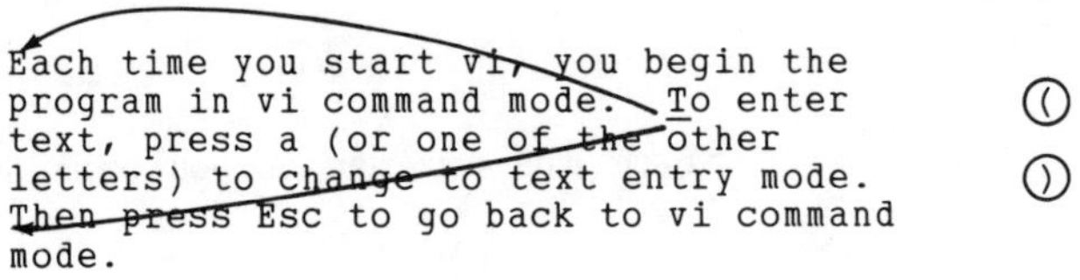

```
Each time you start vi, you begin the
program in vi command mode.  To enter
text, press a (or one of the other
letters) to change to text entry mode.
Then press Esc to go back to vi command
mode.
```

⟮(⟯

⟮)⟯

Figure 6-5. Moving the Cursor One Sentence

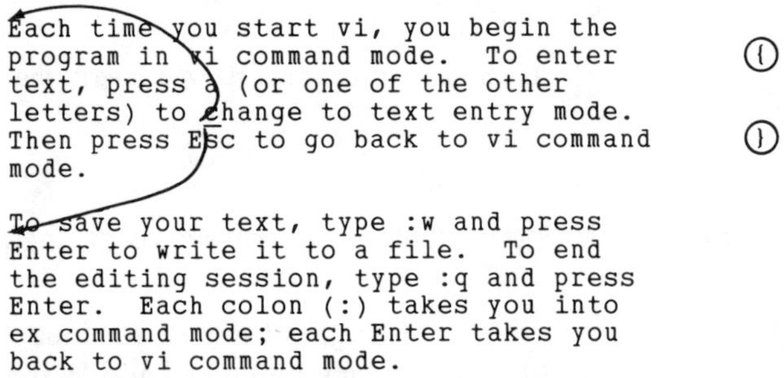

```
Each time you start vi, you begin the
program in vi command mode.  To enter
text, press a (or one of the other
letters) to change to text entry mode.
Then press Esc to go back to vi command
mode.

To save your text, type :w and press
Enter to write it to a file.  To end
the editing session, type :q and press
Enter.  Each colon (:) takes you into
ex command mode; each Enter takes you
back to vi command mode.
```

⟮{⟯

⟮}⟯

Figure 6-6. Moving the Cursor by Paragraphs

To move the cursor by paragraphs, use braces instead of parentheses. In **vi**, a paragraph is understood to be preceded and followed by a blank line. Use a left brace to move back to the beginning of the previous paragraph and a right brace to move forward to the beginning of the next paragraph, as shown in Figure 6-6.

If the cursor is resting on the **c** in *change*, as shown in Figure 6-6, you can press { to move back and } to move forward. Again, you can use multipliers to move the cursor more than one paragraph at a time. In each instance, the cursor will jump to the blank line above the paragraph.

Moving to Areas of the Screen

To move the cursor to a particular location on the screen, without regard to text, you can use one of three mnemonic commands:

H (high)	Top of the screen
M (middle)	Middle of the screen
L (low)	Bottom of the screen

Only capital letters will work here. To move the cursor to the top of the screen, you have to hold down the SHIFT key and type a capital **H**. (Recall that **h** is used to move the cursor one character to the left.) Similarly, you can use **M** to move the cursor to the middle of the screen and **L** to move to the bottom of the screen.

Moving to a Particular Line

Capital letter **G** stands for "Go to line number . . . ." If you type a number in front of **G**, **vi** will place that line number near the middle of the screen, with the cursor resting on the line. No number in front of **G** means "the last line of the document." Here are a few examples:

5G	Move the cursor to line 5
28G	Move the cursor to line 28
G	Move to the last line in this document

While these commands can be handy at times, most people usually don't know line numbers. A related command can help somewhat because it tells you the number of the current line. That may be enough information in many instances. Here is the command:

CTRL G Display the current line number

Each time you press CTRL G, you will see a display of information similar to this:

"sample.doc" [Modified] line 15 of 20 --75%--

These commands have their roots in **vi**'s beginnings as a mode of the line editor **ex**. In a line editor, commands like these are essential; in a full-screen editor, they are not always relevant.

Paging and Scrolling

Paging and scrolling are two ways you can adjust the position of the screen display. Paging is moving the display one page (or full screen) at a time. As with earlier commands, you have one choice for moving back and one for moving forward, as shown in Figure 6-7.

Scrolling in **vi** is similar to paging. The only difference is that, with scrolling, the screen display moves only half a page instead of a full page. The two scrolling commands are:

CTRL U	Scroll up
CTRL D	Scroll down

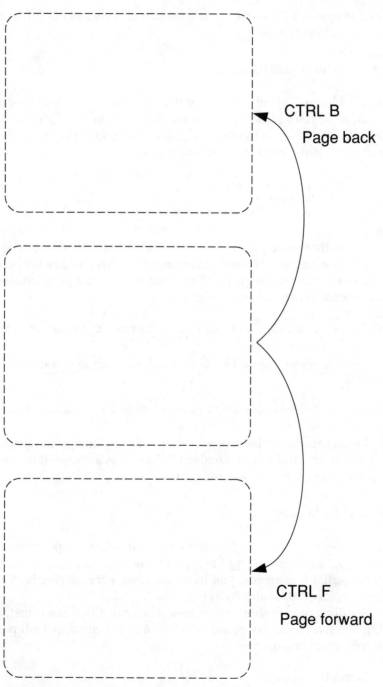

CTRL B
Page back

CTRL F
Page forward

Figure 6-7. Paging

Other Screen Controls

From time to time, either the system or **vi** itself places messages or other visual clutter on your screen. Another control combination allows you to clear these extraneous items from your screen:

CTRL L   Clear messages

We'll conclude this section with three commands for placing the current line (the line on which the cursor is resting). The **z** (zero screen) command, followed by one of three characters, takes care of this adjustment for you:

z ENTER	Move the current line to the top of the screen
z .	Move the current line to the middle of the screen
z −	Move the current line to the bottom of the screen

Unfortunately, these key combinations have no mnemonic meaning. If you want to use them, you'll have to look them up or write them down for quick reference.

Entering Text

At the beginning of this chapter, you learned to type **a** before entering text. Actually, **a** is one of six **vi** commands you can use to enter text. If you're accustomed to working with one of the popular word-processing programs, this may sound like nonsense. But this is the way **vi** works, so this section is devoted to the six different commands that initiate text entry mode. With **vi**, you're supposed to select one of these, basing your selection on the relative location of the new text with respect to the existing text. See Table 6-1 for a summary.

Table 6-1. Text Entry Commands

Action	Commands	Comments
Insert	I or i	Insert new text in front of existing text
Append	A or a	Append new text after existing text
Open	O or o	Open a new line above or below existing text

To summarize from Table 6-1, you *insert* new text to the left of existing text on the same line, *append* new text to the right, and *open* a new line either above or below the current line. Now we'll look at each command in more detail.

Inserting New Text

Use the insert command **i** to insert new text in front of existing text. The new text that you type will be inserted at the location of the cursor, and existing text will be pushed to the right. Here's an example from the second paragraph of **sample.doc**:

1. Move the cursor into position:
   a. Move the cursor to the **b** in **begin** on the first line:

   ```
   Each time you start vi, you begin the
   program in vi command mode.  To enter
   text, press a (or one of the other
   letters) to change to text entry mode.
   Then press Esc to go back to vi command
   mode.
   ```

   b. Press ESC to make sure you're in **vi** command mode.

2. Insert a word in front of **begin**:
   a. Press **i** to request text insertion.
   b. Type **always** (with a space following).
   c. Press ESC to return to **vi** command mode.
   d. Now the paragraph should look like this:

   ```
   Each time you start vi, you always begin the
   program in vi command mode.  To enter
   text, press a (or one of the other
   letters) to change to text entry mode.
   Then press Esc to go back to vi command
   mode.
   ```

To insert new text at the beginning of the current line, you can do one of two things:

- Move the cursor to the beginning of the line (^) and use **i**.
- Leave the cursor where it is and use **I**.

Use the second approach (using **I**) to insert a paragraph number in front of the current paragraph. Repeat steps 1 and 2 above to insert **2.** (with a space following) in front of **Each time**. After you've inserted the number, the paragraph should look like this:

```
2. Each time you start vi, you always begin the
program in vi command mode.  To enter
```

```
text, press a (or one of the other
letters) to change to text entry mode.
Then press Esc to go back to vi command
mode.
```

The paragraph now includes a number at the beginning of the first line and an extra word (*always*). As you can see, the uppercase **I** command isn't really necessary. You can perform any insertion with lowercase **i**.

Appending New Text

The **a** command allows you to append new text to the right of existing text. The new text will be inserted starting in the position following the cursor, and text to the right will be pushed out to make room. You can try this now for yourself.

1. Move the cursor into position:
   a. Move the cursor to the second **t** in **text** on the third line:

   ```
   2. Each time you start vi, you always begin the
   program in vi command mode.  To enter
   text, press a (or one of the other
   letters) to change to text entry mode.
   Then press Esc to go back to vi command
   mode.
   ```

   b. Press ESC to make sure you're in **vi** command mode.

2. Append a word after **text**:
   a. Press **a** to request appending.
   b. Type **freely** (with a space before).
   c. Press ESC to return to **vi** command mode.
   d. Now the paragraph should look like this:

   ```
   2. Each time you start vi, you always begin the
   program in vi command mode.  To enter
   text freely, press a (or one of the other
   letters) to change to text entry mode.
   Then press Esc to go back to vi command
   mode.
   ```

To append new text at the end of the current line, you can do one of two things:

- Move the cursor to the end of the line ($) and use **a**.
- Leave the cursor where it is and use **A**.

Use the second approach (using **A**) to append a word at the end of the current line. Repeat steps 1 and 2 above to append **six** (with a space before) at the end of the line. After you've appended the number, the paragraph should look like this:

```
2. Each time you start vi, you always begin the
program in vi command mode.  To enter
text freely, press a (or one of the other six_
letters) to change to text entry mode.
Then press Esc to go back to vi command
mode.
```

The paragraph now includes two extra words in the third line. You appended one after the cursor with **a** and one at the end of the line with **A**. Again, you could have done both with **a**.

Opening a New Line

You insert and append text on the current line. If you want to add new text on a new line above or below the current line, you can use one of the commands for opening a new line. Here are the commands, which we'll try out below:

- Open a new line above the current line
- Open a new line below the current line

1. Move the cursor into position:
   a. Move the cursor to the **e** in **editor** on the first line:

```
The primary text editor for UNIX is vi
_pronounced vee-eye.  Actually, vi is
nothing more than the visual interpreter
of the ex editor.  When you use vi, you
are really using the ex editor.
```

   b. Press ESC to make sure you're in **vi** command mode.

2. Open a new line above the first line:
   a. Press **O** to open a new line above.
   b. Type **Text Editing in UNIX** and press ENTER to leave a blank line.
   c. Press ESC to return to **vi** command mode.
   d. Now the paragraph should look like this:

```
Text Editing in UNIX


The primary text editor for UNIX is vi
_pronounced vee-eye.  Actually, vi is
nothing more than the visual interpreter
of the ex editor.  When you use vi, you
are really using the ex editor.
```

To open a new line *below* the current line, use lowercase **o**. Repeat Steps 1 and 2 above (but don't press ENTER in Step 2 to leave a blank line) to insert the following new line below the first line of the first paragraph:

(also known as the visual interpreter)

After you've added this line with the **o** command, the paragraph should look like this:

```
Text Editing in UNIX

The primary text editor for UNIX is vi
(also known as the visual interpreter)
-pronounced vee-eye.  Actually, vi is
nothing more than the visual interpreter
of the ex editor.  When you use vi, you
are really using the ex editor.
```

This concludes our discussion of the commands for entering new text. Use **:wq** (or the equivalent **:x**) to save the modified text. You should see a message like

```
"first.doc" 23 liens, 621 characters
```

Summary of Editing Modes

Now that you have learned the six commands for entering text in **vi**, this may be a good time to review the various modes of the editor. When you begin a session, you start out in **vi** command mode, from which you can enter **vi** commands. When you use one of the six text entry commands (**i, I, a, A, o, O**), you change to text entry mode; pressing ESC returns you to **vi** command mode. When you type either **:** or **/**, you change to **ex** command mode; pressing either ESC or ENTER returns you to **vi** command mode. See Figure 6-8 for a pictorial summary.

Deleting Existing Text

During an editing session with **vi**, you can delete characters, words, lines, sentences, and paragraphs, along with parts of words, lines, sentences, and paragraphs. The commands are like the commands for moving the cursor, except that you add the delete command **d**. The exception is the command for deleting characters.

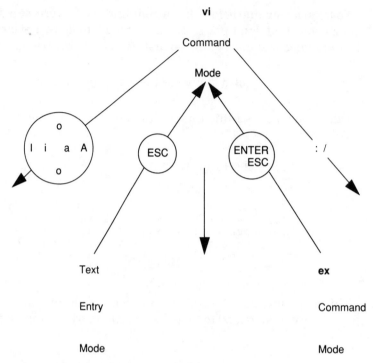

Figure 6-8. Modes Used During Editing

Deleting Characters

To delete one character, move the cursor to the character and press **x**. To delete more than one character, move the cursor to the first character and use a multiplier with **x**. For example, to delete eight characters, use **8x**. Most deletions involve larger amounts of text, and you will probably use **x** most often to delete single characters.

This command illustrates one of the chief complaints about **vi** and UNIX in general: lack of consistency. As you can see here, you have one command for deleting a character (**x**) and another command for deleting larger units of text (**d**).

Deleting Words

To delete one word in **vi** command mode, move the cursor to the first letter of the word and press **dw** (delete word). (If the word to be deleted contains any punctuation, use **dW** instead of **dw**.) To delete more than one word, you can use a multiplier in front of the command. For example, to delete the three words **You don't know**, move the cursor to the **Y** in **You** and press **3dW**. Here is some practice in deleting words. Begin by starting a new editing session with document **sample.doc**; then follow these steps:

1. Move the cursor into position:
   a. Move the cursor to the **2** at the beginning of the second paragraph:

   ```
   2. Each time you start vi, you always begin the
   program in vi command mode.  To enter
   text freely, press a (or one of the other six
   letters) to change to text entry mode.
   Then press ESC to go back to vi command
   mode.
   ```

   b. Press ESC to make sure you're in **vi** command mode.

2. Delete a word:
   a. Press **dW** to delete **2.** .
   b. Advance the cursor to **always** (**5w**) and delete it.
   c. Similarly, delete **freely** and **six** on the third line. (Be sure to restore the comma after **text**.)
   d. This is how the paragraph should look now:

   ```
   Each time you start vi, you begin the
   program in vi command mode.  To enter
   text, press a (or one of the other _
   letters) to change to text entry mode.
   Then press Esc to go back to vi command
   mode.
   ```

3. Delete more than one word:
   a. Move the cursor to the **t** in **time** on the first line.
   b. Press **10dW** to delete ten words.
   c. Press **u** to restore the words deleted.

Whenever you're deleting text, remember the undo command **u**. If you make a mistake, **u** can undo the mistake and restore the text.

Deleting Lines

To delete one line in **vi** command mode, move the cursor to any position on the line and press **dd**. Typing **d** twice means "delete the current line." To delete several lines, you can include a multiplier. Here is some practice in deleting lines:

1. Move the cursor into position:
   a. Move the cursor to the **t** in **the** on the second line of the first paragraph:

   ```
   Text Editing in UNIX

   The primary text editor for UNIX is vi
   (also known as the visual interpreter)
   —pronounced vee-eye.  Actually, vi is
   nothing more than the visual interpreter
   of the ex editor.  When you use vi, you
   are really using the ex editor.
   ```

   b. Press ESC to make sure you're in **vi** command mode.

2. Delete a single line:
   a. Press **dd** to delete the entire line.
   b. You will see the line disappear and the cursor wind up on the next line.

3. Delete three lines at once:
   a. Without moving the cursor, press **3dd** to delete three lines.
   b. Press **u** to restore the three lines.
   c. The paragraph should look like this:

   ```
   Text Editing in UNIX

   The primary text editor for UNIX is vi
   —pronounced vee-eye.  Actually, vi is
   nothing more than the visual interpreter
   of the ex editor.  When you use vi, you
   are really using the ex editor.
   ```

If the cursor is resting somewhere within the ends of a line, you can also do a couple of variations. You can use **d^** to delete all text from the cursor to the beginning of the line, or you can use **d$** to delete all text from the cursor to the end of the line. You can practice using these variations a couple of times if you wish. Be sure to restore any text deleted with **u**.

Deleting Sentences

To delete an entire sentence, move the cursor to the beginning of the sentence and press **d)**. To delete more than one sentence, you can include a multiplier in front of the command. For example, to delete three sentences at once, position the cursor and press **3d)**. Here is some practice in deleting sentences:

1. Move the cursor into position:
   a. Move the cursor to the **A** in **Actually** on the third line of the first paragraph:

```
Text Editing in UNIX

The primary text editor for UNIX is vi
(also known as the visual interpreter)
—pronounced vee-eye.  Actually, vi is
nothing more than the visual interpreter
of the ex editor.  When you use vi, you
are really using the ex editor.
```

b. Press ESC to make sure you're in **vi** command mode.

2. Delete a single sentence:
   a. Press **d)** to delete the sentence.
   b. You will see the sentence disappear and the cursor wind up in the next sentence.
   c. Press **u** to restore the sentence.

3. Delete two sentences at once:
   a. Without moving the cursor, press **2d)** to delete two sentences.
   b. Press **u** to restore the two sentences.

Since you restored the deleted text, the paragraph should be the same now. You can delete part of a sentence about the same way you can delete part of a line. Move the cursor to the desired location in the sentence and press one of these:

d(Delete all text from the cursor to the beginning of the sentence
d)   Delete all text from the cursor to the end of the sentence

Deleting Paragraphs

To delete one paragraph, move the cursor to the blank line above the paragraph and press d } . To delete more than one paragraph, you can use a multiplier with the command. For example, to delete three paragraphs, position the cursor and press **3d }** .

1. Move the cursor into position:
   a. Move the cursor to the blank line above the first paragraph:

```
Text Editing in UNIX

The primary text editor for UNIX is vi
(also known as the visual interpreter)
—pronounced vee-eye.  Actually, vi is
nothing more than the visual interpreter
of the ex editor.  When you use vi, you
are really using the ex editor.
```

   b. Press ESC to make sure you're in **vi** command mode.

2. Delete a single paragraph:
   a. Press **d }** to delete the paragraph.
   b. You will see the paragraph disappear.
   c. Press **u** to restore the paragraph.

3. Delete three paragraphs at once:
   a. Without moving the cursor, press **3d)** to delete all three paragraphs.
   b. Press **u** to restore the three paragraphs.

Since you restored the deleted text, the document should be the same now. You can delete part of a paragraph about the same way you can delete part of a line. Move the cursor to the desired location in the paragraph and press one of the following:

d {	Delete all text from the cursor to the beginning of the paragraph
d }	Delete all text from the cursor to the end of the paragraph

This concludes our discussion of deleting text. As you can see, deleting characters is the exception. Otherwise, each command for deleting a unit of text is identical to the command for moving the cursor the same amount, with the addition of **d** (delete). You can even use multipliers in the same way.

Moving Text

Moving text from one location in a document is very similar to deleting text. In both instances, the text disappears from view. However, during a move, the text is stored in a buffer until you're ready to retrieve it. To move any unit of text from location X to location Y, follow these four general steps:

- Move the cursor to location X.
- Delete the text, using one of the commands described in the previous section.
- Move the cursor to location Y.
- Insert the text at the new location, using a "put" command.

We won't repeat all the different commands for deleting text in this section. Instead, we'll focus on sentences here, leaving the rest for a summary. The key command in any move is the **put** command, which, like many other **vi** commands, comes in two varieties:

P	Insert text in front of the cursor or above the current line
p	Append text after the cursor or below the current line

You could say that uppercase **P** corresponds to **I**, **i**, and **O**, while lowercase **p** corresponds to **a**, **A**, and **o**. You have to choose one of the two, depending on the context.

Moving Sentences

We'll choose a sentence from the first paragraph to be moved to another paragraph, following the general steps shown at the beginning of this section. Here are the four steps in detail:

1. Move the cursor into position:
   a. Move the cursor to the **A** in **Actually** on the third line of the first paragraph:

   ```
   Text Editing in UNIX

   The primary text editor for UNIX is vi
   (also known as the visual interpreter)
   —pronounced vee-eye.  Actually, vi is
   nothing more than the visual interpreter
   of the ex editor.  When you use vi, you
   are really using the ex editor.
   ```

   b. Press ESC to make sure you're in **vi** command mode.

2. Delete a sentence from its current location:
   a. Press **d)** to delete the sentence.
   b. The sentence will vanish, and the paragraph will look like this:

   ```
   Text Editing in UNIX

   The primary text editor for UNIX is vi
   (also known as the visual interpreter)
   —pronounced vee-eye.  _
   @
   When you use vi, you
   are really using the ex editor.
   ```

3. Move the cursor to the target location:
   a. Move the cursor to the **T** in **Then** on the fifth line of the second paragraph.
   b. The paragraph should look like this:

   ```
   Each time you start vi, you begin the
   program in vi command mode.  To enter
   text, press a (or one of the other
   letters) to change to text entry mode.
   Then press Esc to go back to vi command
   mode.
   ```

4. Insert (or put) the sentence here:
   a. Press uppercase **P** to insert the sentence.
   b. The paragraph should now look like this:

```
Each time you start vi, you begin the
program in vi command mode.  To enter
text, press a (or one of the other
letters) to change to text entry mode.
Actually, vi is
nothing more than the visual interpreter
of the ex editor.  Then press Esc to go back to vi
command
mode.
```

You have just moved a sentence from the first paragraph to the second. Now, to make sure you are familiar with the procedure, repeat steps 1–4 to move the sentence back to its original location. This time, however, use **p** in step 4 instead of **P**.

Moving Other Amounts of Text

A small-scale, but sometimes important, move is the transposition of two adjacent characters in a word. To transpose two characters, move the cursor to the first of the two and press **xp**. For example, suppose you typed **visaul** instead of **visual** in the first paragraph. Your first step is to move the cursor to the **a** in **visaul**, so that the word looks like this: **visaul**. Now press **xp** and you have this: **visual**.

You can move a word (or a series of words) from one place to another by deleting the word (or words) at the current location, moving the cursor to the new location, and putting them there. For example, to move **the visual interpreter**, move the cursor to the **t** in **the**, press **3dw**, move the cursor to the new location, and press **P** (to insert) or **p** (to append).

For lines of text, begin by deleting the lines with **dd**, **d^**, **d$**, **5dd**, or whatever is appropriate. Then move to the target location and press **P** or **p**. For paragraphs, begin by deleting the paragraphs with **d{**, **d}**, **d3}**, or whatever is best. Then put the paragraphs in the desired location, as described above.

Finding and Replacing Text

Searching and replacing are functions of **ex**. To search forward for text, press slash (/), enter the desired search string, and press ENTER to return to **vi** command mode. If a match is found, the cursor will jump to the first occurrence of the string. To search for the next occurrence, press **n** (next) as many times as needed. Here is an example of a search for text. If necessary, return the cursor to the first line of the document (**1G**); then follow these steps:

1. Begin the search:
   a. Type **/editor** and press ENTER.
   b. The cursor will jump to the **e** in **editor** on the first line of the first paragraph.

   ```
   Text Editing in UNIX

   The primary text editor for UNIX is vi
   (also known as the visual interpreter)
   —pronounced vee-eye.  Actually, vi is
   nothing more than the visual interpreter
   of the ex editor.  When you use vi, you
   are really using the ex editor.
   ```

2. Continue the search:
   a. Press **n** (next).
   b. The cursor will jump to the next occurrence of **editor**:

   ```
   Text Editing in UNIX

   The primary text editor for UNIX is vi
   (also known as the visual interpreter)
   —pronounced vee-eye.  Actually, vi is
   nothing more than the visual interpreter
   of the ex editor.  When you use vi, you
   are really using the ex editor.
   ```

   c. Continue pressing **n** a few more times.

The cursor will continue jumping to subsequent occurrences of **editor**. To continue searching for the same string in the opposite direction (backward), press **N** instead of **n**. In this document, it probably doesn't make any difference, but to avoid words like **editors**, **editorial**, and so on, type a space after the **r** in **editor** at the beginning of the search.

To search backward in the document instead of forward, use this search command instead of the one shown in Step 1 above:

```
?editor
```

The question mark (**?**) means, "Search backward," while the slash (/) means, "Search forward." When you search backward, you can still use **n** and **N** to continue searching. However, the search directions for **n** and **N** are reversed when you search with a question mark (**?**).

Replacing Text

Like word-processing programs, **vi** (actually **ex**) allows you to search for text and replace it with different text. In this way, you can correct spelling errors and change terminology in one of your documents. A command to replace text begins with a colon (:) to switch to **ex** command mode. Next, type the beginning line number, a comma, and the ending line number. Then type the name of the command, **s** (substitute), a slash (/), the search string, another slash (/), the replacement string, and a final slash (/). If you want all occurrences of the string to be replaced in each line, you can also append **g** (for global) at the end of the command. Here is a summary:

```
:begin,ends/search/replace/g

where

:           means this is an ex command
begin       is the beginning line number
end         is the ending line number
s           is the name of the command (substitute)
search      is the search string (the text you're looking for)
replace     is the replacement string (the text that replaces
            the search string)
g           is the global indicator (replace all occurrences
            on each line, not just the first)
```

In the following example, we'll change each occurrence of **vi** to **VI**. Begin by returning the cursor to the first line of the document (using **1G** if necessary); then follow these steps:

1. Change **vi** to **VI** everywhere in the document:
    a. Type the following command and press ENTER:

        ```
        :1,$s/vi/VI/g
        ```

    b. The first paragraph should look like this:

        ```
        Text Editing in UNIX

        The primary text editor for UNIX is VI
        (also known as the VIsual interpreter)
        _pronounced vee-eye.  Actually, VI is
        nothing more than the VIsual interpreter
        of the ex editor.  When you use VI, you
        are really using the ex editor.
        ```

2. Change **VI** back to **vi** again:
    a. Type the following command and press ENTER:

        ```
        :1,$s?VI?vi?g
        ```

    b. The first paragraph should look like this:

```
Text Editing in UNIX

The primary text editor for UNIX is vi
(also known as the visual interpreter)
—pronounced vee-eye.  Actually, vi is
nothing more than the visual interpreter
of the ex editor.  When you use vi, you
are really using the ex editor.
```

In step 1, note that the command made all the desired replacements, but also changed **visual** to **VIsual**. This was unavoidable in this example because at least one occurrence of **vi** was followed by a comma, meaning that we couldn't leave a space after **vi** in the search command.

You can use the beginning and ending line numbers at the beginning of the search command to restrict the search. In the examples above, we searched the entire document from the first line (1) to the last ($). You can use numbers, search strings, or symbols like . (current line) or **$** (last line) for line numbers. Here are a few more examples of beginning and ending line numbers that you could use in a search command:

5,.	Search from line 5 to the current line.
.,/new/	Search from the current line to the first line that contains the word **new**.
/new/,/old	Search from the first line that contains **new** to the first line that contains **old**.
.-10,$	Search from 10 lines behind the current line to the end of the document.

As the example shown above illustrates, you can search either forward (**/**) or backward (**?**) in a substitution command. We searched backward in step 2 because the cursor was near the end of the document as a result of the first search.

CHAPTER 7

FORMATTING TEXT

Introduction

If you've been using a word-processing program like WordPerfect on your DOS system, then you're used to having text-editing and text-formatting combined in one program. All the features for formatting the printed output are found in the same program that allows you to create and update documents. In UNIX, however, these two general functions are separate: text-editing is performed by **vi**, while formatting is performed by a suite of programs, which we'll examine in this chapter.

The Primary Programs

UNIX formatting got started in the late 1960s with a modest program from the Massachesetts Institute of Technology (MIT) called **roff** (short for runoff). Joseph Ossanna of Bell Laboratories enhanced **roff**, and the result was **nroff** (short for new runoff). Additional enhancements to accommodate a photo-typesetting machine produced a third product called **troff** (short for typesetter runoff).

The **nroff** program (pronounced "en-roff") produces typewriter-like characters of fixed width for line printers and daisy-wheel printers. Although **nroff** includes a variety of features for adjusting text on a printed page, it lacks the ability to handle proportional spacing.

The **troff** program (pronounced "tee-roff") produces characters of variable widths for laser printers and phototypesetters. The program has all the features of **nroff**, with the addition of the ability to produce proportional spacing and multiple fonts.

Like the WordStar program for microcomputers and the SCRIPT program for mainframes, **nroff** and **troff** both rely on commands embedded in the main text. These embedded commands, known as **requests**, have mnemonic names like **.ll** (line length). Most requests, like **.ll**, begin with periods and identify themselves with two letters. Many requests also support different kinds of arguments. In short, these requests look remarkably similar to Word-Star's famous (or infamous) dot commands.

If you're used to a formatting program that allows you to select formatting features from a menu, you may be wondering whether or not the UNIX programs represent a step backward. These programs, developed in the late 1960s and the 1970s may seem fairly primitive next to PageMaker, FrameMaker, or Ventura Publisher. The main disadvantage of the UNIX programs is that they don't allow you to see what a given page will look like until you print it.

Other Formatting Programs

While **nroff** and **troff** are the primary formatting tools of the UNIX system, they are not alone. Because **nroff** and **troff** support **macros**, anyone can construct another program derived from them, building on the basic requests they provide. In fact, people have done this a number of times, creating **macro packages** from **nroff** and **troff**. In general, a macro package is a parallel program designed for a specific purpose. It is parallel because it often provides many of the same features that **nroff** and **troff** themselves provide. But because the individual macros in a macro package combine so many basic atomic requests, macro packages are generally easier to use. Here are three of the most widely used macro packages:

ms	Standard with UNIX Version 7
me	Standard with Berkeley versions of UNIX
mm	Standard with UNIX System V (described in this chapter)

Preprocessors handle specialized tasks for **nroff** and **troff**. Four of the most widely used preprocessors are as follows:

tbl	Formats tabular material for both programs
neqn	Formats equations for **nroff**
eqn	Formats equations for **troff**
pic	Formats graphical material for **troff**

Finally, there are the miscellaneous utilities:

checkeq	Checks usage for **neqn** and **eqn**
deroff	Removes all formatting requests from a file

The mm Macro Package

The **mm** macro package will be the main subject of this chapter. This is a good place to start because **mm** is quite a bit easier to use than **nroff** and **troff**. To produce printed output with **mm**, you go through three general steps, although the first two may not be completely separate. Here is an example for a document called **report**:

- Enter the main text with **vi**
- Embed the formatting requests in the main text
- Process the document using one of the following command lines:

```
$ mm [option(s)] report
```

or

```
$ nroff -cm [option(s)] report
```

or

```
$ troff -cm [option(s)] report
```

By piping the output to a screen display program like **pg** or **more**, you can preview a document without printing it. Here is an example:

```
$ mm report ¦ more
```

A document formatted by **mm** prints with the following defaults unless you change them in **mm**:

- ¾-inch offset for the left margin
- 10 characters per inch (pica)
- 60 characters per line (6 inches)
- Six lines per inch

This covers the general information about **mm**. Now we'll begin describing specific features, including paragraphs, display text, lists, highlighting, spacing, and changing point size. In the examples shown in this chapter, you will see the input document with its formatting requests on the left and the printed output on the right.

Paragraphs

Since **vi** doesn't have word wrap, you have to press ENTER at the end of every line, even when you're in the middle of a paragraph. The **.P** request tells **mm** that the lines belong together as a single paragraph. You can type the lines as long or as short as you like, and **mm** will **fill** each line to fit the current margins. You must precede each paragraph with a new **.P** request, which offers you two choices.

Block Paragraph

To form a block paragraph, without an indented first line, type **.P 0** (dot P space zero) on a blank line above the first line. (You can also use **.P**.)

Your Document	Printed Output
.P ☐ A block paragraph looks like this. It doesn't have any indentation.	A block paragraph looks like this. It doesn't have any indentation.

Indented Paragraph

To form a paragraph whose first line is indented, type **.P 1** (dot P space one) on a blank line above the first line.

Your Document	Printed Output
.P 1 A typical paragraph looks like this. The first line is indented, but the rest of the lines aren't.	A typical paragraph looks like this. The first line is indented, but the rest of the lines aren't.

Display Text

You can set special text apart from ordinary text by displaying it on the printed page in a different format. Your document may contain a quotation, a poem, or some other text that is out of the ordinary. The **mm** program gives you a choice of four different formats for display text, which we'll explore in this section.

You can also choose between two different ways of handling the text that surrounds the display text. With either choice, if the display text doesn't fit on the current page, **mm** will move it to the following page. If you have a *static display*, you leave a gap on the previous page where part of the display text would have been. In a *floating display*, ordinary text that follows the display in your document is allowed to fill the gap on the preceding page. The three requests for creating displays are as follows:

.DS	Begin a static display
.DF	Begin a floating display
.DE	End a display (static or floating)

We'll use **.DS** in the examples that follow, but you can substitute **.DF** for **.DS** if you prefer.

Indented Display

To display text by indenting it five spaces, add the indent argument **I** to the **.DS** (or **.DF**) request, as shown here:

Your Document	Printed Output

<pre>.P 1
Here is a quotation set
apart from ordinary text:
.DS I
"Their way of life
faded away and they were
eventually forgotten."
.DE
.P 1
The author concluded his
book with these words.</pre>
	<pre> Here is a quotation set
	apart from ordinary text:
	
	        "Their way of life faded
	        away and they were
	        eventually forgotten."
	
	    The author concluded his
	book with these words.</pre>

Double-Indented Display

To display text by indenting it from both margins, add the indent (**I**) and fill (**F**) arguments to the **.DS** (or **.DF**) request. The fill argument requires a number n to indicate the number of spaces to be indented from the right margin. In the following example, we'll leave five spaces:

Your Document	Printed Output
| ```
.P 1
Here is a quotation set
apart from ordinary text:
.DS I F 5
"Their way of life
faded away and they were
eventually forgotten."
.DE
.P 1
The author concluded his
book with these words.
``` | Here is a quotation set<br>apart from ordinary text:<br><br>"Their way of life<br>faded away and they<br>were eventually<br>forgotten."<br><br>The author concluded his<br>book with these words. |

Centered Display

To display text by centering it, add the center argument **C** to your **.DS** (or **.DF**) request. As the following example shows, this can be an appropriate way to display poetry or a title.

Your Document	Printed Output
| ```
.P 1
Next he referred to the
following work:
.DS C
"Sailing Along"
by
Admiral Wave
.DE
.P 1
Then he continued his
discussion of nautical
history.
``` | Next he referred to the<br>following work:<br><br>"Sailing Along"<br>by<br>Admiral Wave<br><br>Then he continued his<br>discussion of nautical<br>history. |

Blocked Display

The blocked display is a variation of the centered display; the text is centered with left-justification. To display text in this way, add the center block argument **CB** to your **.DS** (or **.DF**) request. Here is an example of a blocked display:

Your Document	Printed Output
| ```
.P 1
He quoted the words of
Paul of Tarsus:
.DS CB
When I was a child,
I spake as a child,
I understood as a child,
I thought as a child.
.DE
.P 1
Then he talked about his
travels through the
ancient world.
``` | ```
      He quoted the words of
Paul of Tarsus:

      When I was a child,
      I spake as a child,
      I understood as a child,
      I thought as a child.

            Then he talked about his
travels through the ancient
world.
``` |

Lists

Many different types of documents require lists of various items. With **mm**, you can set up a list in which each item begins with a bullet, a hyphen, a letter, a number, or a word. Although a different request begins each type of list, the same list item request **.LI** begins each individual item and the same list end request **.LE** ends each completed list. Now we'll examine the six types of lists supported by **mm**.

Bullet List

To set up a list with each item following a bullet, use the bullet list request **.BL**. If you run **mm** under **nroff**, each bullet will appear as a plus sign printed over a lowercase o; if you run **mm** under **troff**, each bullet will be a real bullet. Here is an example of a bullet list:

Your Document	Printed Output
| ```
.P 1
The procedure for setting up
a list with mm is as follows:
.BL
.LI
Identify the type of list
.LI
Enter the individual list
items
.LI
End the completed list
.LE
``` | ```
      The procedure for setting
up a list with mm is as
follows:

    • Identify the type of
      list

    • Enter the individual
      list items

    • End the completed list
``` |

Dash List

This style is just like a bullet list, except that each item is preceded by a hyphen instead of a bullet. (It's really a hyphen, not a dash.) For this style, use the dash list request **.DL**. Here is an example:

Your Document	*Printed Output*
| ```
.P 1
The procedure for setting up
a list with mm is as follows:
.DL
.LI
Identify the type of list
.LI
Enter the individual list
items
.LI
End the completed list
.LE
``` | The procedure for setting up a list with mm is as follows:<br><br>   – Identify the type of list<br><br>   – Enter the individual list items<br><br>   – End the completed list |

Mark List

This style is just like a bullet list or a dash list, except that you choose the character that precedes each item. For this style, use the mark list request **.ML**, followed by the character (or characters) desired. In this example, we'll precede each item with an asterisk (*):

Your Document	*Printed Output*
| ```
.P 1
The procedure for setting up
a list with mm is as follows:
.ML *
.LI
Identify the type of list
.LI
Enter the individual list
items
.LI
End the completed list
.LE
``` | The procedure for setting up a list with mm is as follows:<br><br>   * Identify the type of list<br><br>   * Enter the individual list items<br><br>   * End the completed list |

Reference List

A bibliography is an example of a numbered list of references. To list a sequence of references by number, you can use the reference list request **.RL**. The list that results will be like the lists in the previous three examples, but **mm** will number the items for you automatically. Here is an example of a reference list:

Your Document	Printed Output
| ```
.P 1
Here is a list of the works
cited in this book:
.RL
.LI
Anthony, Rufus, "You Can't
Get Any Better''
.LI
Butler, Abigail, "You Can
Be the Best''
.LI
Colter, Billy, "How to
Be Acceptable''
.LE
``` | ```
   Here is a list of the
works cited in this book:

[1] Anthony, Rufus, "You
    Can't Get Any Better"

[2] Butler, Abigail, "You
    Can Be the Best"

[3] Colter, Billy, "How to
    Be Acceptable"
``` |

Variable-Item List

A glossary is an example of a variable-item list. Each item begins with a different word, which is followed by a definition. Although different combinations are possible, we'll refer to the two parts of a variable-item list as the term and the definition. To form such a list, use the variable-item list request **.VL**.

Immediately following the request, you have to type a number, which indicates how much space is required for your terms. More precisely, the number gives the number of columns between the left margin and the starting point of each definition or explanation. (The number you choose must be a minimum of two greater than the number of characters in the longest term in your list.) In the following example, we'll use 5.

One difference between a variable-item list and all the other types relates to the way you enter the individual items. You have to type the desired term immediately after each **.LI** request. The term becomes the leader, while the definition becomes the body of the item. Here is an example:

Your Document	Printed Output
| ```
.P 1
Here is a list of common
household pets:
.VL 5
.LI cat
Perfect for people who
don't mind a pet with
an independent spirit.
.LI dog
Best for people who
require obedience
and full loyalty.
.LE
``` | ```
    Here is a list of common
household pets:

cat Perfect for people who
    don't mind a pet with an
    independent spirit.

dog Best for people who
    require obedience
    and full loyalty.
``` |

Auto-Number List

Without an argument, an auto-number list is very much like a reference list. The items are automatically numbered in sequence. Here is an example of an auto-number list with no argument:

Your Document	Printed Output
| ```
.P 1
Here is a list of the works
cited in this book:
.AL
.LI
Anthony, Rufus, "You Can't
Get Any Better"
.LI
Butler, Abigail, "You Can
Be the Best"
.LI
Colter, Billy, "How to
Be Acceptable"
.LE
``` | ```
    Here is a list of the
works cited in this book:

1. Anthony, Rufus, "You
   Can't Get Any Better"

2. Butler, Abigail, "You
   Can Be the Best"

3. Colter, Billy, "How to
   Be Acceptable"
``` |

In the example shown above, the output is nearly identical to the output for the **.VL** request. However, you also have the option of requesting other numbering schemes, using either letters of the alphabet or Roman numerals. To make a selection, type one of the following letters after the **.AL** request:

A	Choose uppercase letters (A, B, C, ...)
a	Choose lowercase letters (a, b, c, ...)
I	Choose uppercase Roman numerals (I, II, III, ...)
i	Choose lowercase Roman numerals (i, ii, iii, ...)

In the next example, we'll use lowercase letters for numbering:

Your Document	Printed Output

```
.P 1
Here is a list of the works        Here is a list of the
cited in this book:            works cited in this book:
.AL a
.LI                             a. Anthony, Rufus, "You
Anthony, Rufus, "You Can't         Can't Get Any Better"
Get Any Better"
.LI                             b. Butler, Abigail, "You
Butler, Abigail, "You Can          Can Be the Best"
Be the Best"
.LI                             c. Colter, Billy, "How to
Colter, Billy, "How to             Be Acceptable"
Be Acceptable"
.LE
```

By choosing more than one numbering scheme and nesting **.AL** requests, you can construct an outline. Select **I** for the first **.AL** request (the first level of the outline), **A** for the second, **1** for the third, **i** for the fourth, and so on. The numbering for any given level continues until its **.LE** request appears. Here is an example of a simple outline constructed from successive **.AL** requests:

Your Document	Printed Output

```
.AL I    [Start of Roman list]   I.    Introduction
.LI
Introduction                     II.   Body
.LI
Body                                   A.   Beginning
.AL A    [Start of "ABC" list]
.LI                                    B.   Middle
Beginning
.LI                                         1. Features
Middle
.AL 1    [Start of "123" list]              2. Advantages
.LI
Features                               C.   End
.LI
Advantages                       III. Conclusion
.LE    [End of "123" list]
.LI
End
.LE    [End of "ABC" list]
.LI
Conclusion
.LE    [End of Roman list]
```

Once you've set up an outline like this, you can insert new items or remove old items, and **mm** will renumber them for you automatically.

Other Features

Now you've learned the major features of **mm**: paragraphs, displays, and lists. In the rest of this chapter, we'll consider several additional features: justifying text, skipping lines, highlighting text, and changing point size.

Justifying Text

Unless you give **mm** a specific request to do so, **mm** does not line up text at the right margin. (Aligning text at a margin is called *justification*.) To turn on justification at the right margin, embed a side alignment request, **.SA 1**. To turn off justification again and return to **mm**'s default, use **.SA 0**. Below is a simple example.

Your Document	Printed Output
| ```
.SA 1
.P 1
When you justify text, you
align it at a margin. Most
printed text is justified at
the left margin. A lot of
text is also justified at
the right margin.
.SA 0
.P 1
This paragraph is justified
at the left margin, but not
at the right margin. This is
sometimes called ragged right.
``` | ```
   When you justify text,
you align it at a margin. Most
printed text is justified
at the left margin. A lot of
text is also justified at the
right margin.

   This paragraph is
justified at the left margin,
but not at the right margin.
This is sometimes called
ragged right.
``` |

Right-justification, the traditional approach to printing, tends to present a more formal appearance. In recent years, however, the ragged right look has been growing more and more fashionable, especially among graphic designers. Ragged right text is said to look more natural to the reader, and graphic designers find a rough edge more interesting to look at than a straight line. There are no fixed rules, but in general, most newspapers use right-justification, while magazines and advertisements use ragged right.

Skipping Lines

With most word-processing programs, you can leave blank space on a page by pressing ENTER the desired number of times. With **mm**, you have a request that leaves space for you. Just embed the space request, **.SP n**, with a number to indicate the number of blank lines desired. In the following example, we'll leave three blank lines after a title.

Your Document	Printed Output
| ```
.DS C
The Ride Home
.DE
.SP 3
.P 1
The clouds had settled in
over the valley, and the
coming of evening had
made the trail harder
than ever to find.
``` | ```
The Ride Home



    The clouds had settled in
over the valley, and the
coming of evening had made the
trail harder than ever to
find.
``` |

After the title, **mm** skips three lines before starting the opening paragraph.

Highlighting Text

When you use a word-processing program, you probably have a key that you can press to start bold or underscoring. With **mm**, you have three requests available:

.B	Begin bold
.I	Begin italic (or underscoring)
.R	End bold or italic (begin roman)

Under **nroff**, italic really means underscoring; under **troff**, you get true italic characters.

To highlight a single word, enter a new line that contains the request and the word by themselves. For a single word, you don't need the **.R** request to end highlighting. Here is how you would make the word **frequent** bold:

```
.B frequent
```

To highlight more than one word, enter the start request (**.B** or **.I**) on a separate line, enter the words on the next line, and enter the end request (**.R**) on another separate line. Here is how you would make the words **an entire day** italic (or underscored):

```
.I
an entire day
.R
```

When highlighting several words, you have to bracket the words between a pair of requests, as shown above. This can make your document look disjointed and fragmented, but **mm** will pick up the pieces and reconstruct your paragraph for you. Here is an example of a couple of paragraphs that contain highlighted words:

Your Document	Printed Output
| ```
.P 1
To make a word
.B bold
, use the .B request by
itself. For
.B
a few words
.R
, bracket the words on
separate lines with the .B
and .R requests.
.P 1
To
.I underscore
a word, use the .I request
by itself. For
.I
a few words
.R
, bracket the words on
separate lines with the .I
and .R requests.
``` | To make a word **bold,** use the .B request by itself. For **a few words,** bracket the words on separate lines with the .B and .R requests.<br><br>To _underscore_ a word, use the .I request by itself. For _a few words,_ bracket the words on separate lines with the .I and .R requests. |

If a word is followed by punctuation, such as a comma or a period, be sure to exclude the punctuation from highlighting, as shown in the paragraphs above. This makes your on-screen document look a little strange, but it keeps your printed page from looking even stranger.

Changing Point Size

Typesetters measure the size of a set of characters in _points_, one point equaling $1/72$ of an inch. For a given set of characters, the point size is defined as the distance from the bottom of a lowercase p to the top of an uppercase letter. Most ordinary text is printed at 10 points (elite on a typewriter), 11 points, or 12 points (pica on a typewriter).

Vertical spacing, also measured in points, is defined as the distance from the bottom of one line of text to the bottom of the next. Vertical spacing is usually about 20% greater than the point size of the characters. The difference between point size and vertical spacing is called _leading_ (pronounced like heading).

An illustration of point size, vertical spacing, and leading is shown in Figure 7-1. Here, the point size is 10 points, the vertical spacing is 12 points, and the leading is two points (the defaults for **troff**).
```

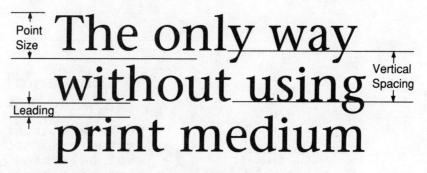

Figure 7-1 Point Size, Vertical Spacing, and Leading

When you are processing **mm** requests under **troff**, you can use the **.S** request to change point size or vertical spacing (or both in the same request). The general format of this request is as follows:

.S *p* *v*

where *p* is an optional point size and *v* is an optional vertical spacing. You can include either of the arguments alone or both together.

Here is how you would change to a point size of 14 and a vertical spacing of 17:

.S 14 17

Assuming the defaults are currently in effect, the preceding example is equivalent to the following:

.S +4 +5

The two previous examples illustrate the use of absolute numbers and relative numbers. A third possibility is to use one of the mnemonic letters in place of numbers. The mnemonic letters are as follows:

P   Previous settings
C   Current settings
D   Default settings

The first letter (**P**), when added to the **.S** request, is equivalent to using **.S** alone without any arguments.

This example shows how to change point size and vertical spacing several times in a document:

Your Document	Printed Output
| ```
.SP 3
.DS C
.S 14 17
Hot shot
.S -2 -3
By Bud Rowe
.DE
.S D
.P 0
He knew what he wanted.  He
took what he wanted.  He
kept what he took.  He was
a hot shot.
``` | Hot shot<br>By Bud Rowe<br><br>He knew what he wanted.  He wanted.  He took what he wanted.  He kept what he took. He was a hot shot. |

Here is a summary of the **mm** requests in the previous example:

.SP 3	Skip down three lines
.DS C	Start a centered display
.S 14 17	Increase the point size to 14 points and the vertical spacing to 17 points
.S −2 −3	Decrease the point size by two points and the vertical spacing by three
.DE	End the centered display
.S D	Restore the defaults (point size = 10 points, vertical spacing = 12 points)
.P 0	Start a block paragraph
```

CHAPTER 8

HANDLING COMMUNICATION

To a DOS user, communication means buying a modem, buying software like ProComm or CrossTalk, and logging into bulletin boards. While logged in, the user may read notices, download programs, and even upload programs into the bulletin board. The user may also call up other users and send messages and files back and forth. In DOS, communication takes place under application programs; it is not indigenous to the operating system check.

In UNIX, communication is built into the operating system (but the system administrator has to do a lot of work to get it working). If you are using a UNIX system, you already have access to programs that allow you to send and receive messages and files within your own system and outside your system. Since UNIX is a multiuser system, it includes facilities that allow one user to reach another—either on the same system or on another system. In addition, there is an international bulletin board available to UNIX users.

The UNIX programs described in this chapter have no DOS counterparts. We'll explore three areas: internal communication, external communication, and the bulletin board. Some UNIX commands overlap two or three of these areas, but most commands relate primarily to one area only.

Internal Communication

For communication within a single system, UNIX provides three facilities for users: terminal-to-terminal communication, automatic reminder service, and electronic mail. Let's take a look at each of the UNIX facilities.

Terminal-to-Terminal Communication

If you want to send a message directly from your terminal to another user's terminal, you can use the **write** command. For example, suppose there is another user on your system named Bill (login name **bill**). If you have an urgent message for Bill, you can send it to him quickly in the following way:

```
$ write bill
I need to see you right away. -o
CTRL D [not displayed]
$ _
```

If Bill's terminal allows messages, the following will appear on his screen immediately:

```
Message from don (tty09) [Mon Jul 26 10:17:52]...
I need to see you right away. -o
<EOT>
```

If Bill is working at his terminal when this message appears on his screen, he can respond with another **write** command back to Don:

```
$ write don
OK.  I can be in your office by 10:30. -oo
CTRL D [not displayed]
$ _
```

Don will see something like the following on his screen:

```
Message from bill (tty11) [Mon Jul 26 10:18:23]...
OK. I can be in your office by 10:30. -oo
<EOT>
```

A simple protocol makes it clear to the recipient when your message (or the entire dialogue) is finished. Then the recipient doesn't have to wonder whether or not the sender is about to say more. You can type **-o** at the end of a message to mean "over" and **-oo** at the end of a dialogue to mean "over and out."

When you send a message with the **write** command, it appears on the recipient's screen, overwriting anything that may already be on the screen. If you are in the middle of an important project and you can't be interrupted by **write** messages, you can use the **mesg** command to turn them off. Just include the no option (**n**), as shown here:

```
$ mesg n
$ _
```

Later, when the project has been completed, you can allow messages again by including the yes option (**y**) in another **mesg** command:

```
$ mesg y
$ _
```

Self Reminders

The **calendar** command provides an electronic reminder service. Approximately once a day, a system utility searches each user's home directory for a file named **calendar**. You can store reminders for yourself in this file, so that the file looks like this sample:

```
$ cat calendar
Sep 5      Monday at 9:30      Staff meeting
Sep 6      Tuesday at 2:00     Report on sales due
Sep 9      Friday at 3:00      Party for Cindy
Sep 15     Thursday at 12:00   Lunch with Paul and Steve
$ _
```

The **calendar** command will scan your file for you, identify each line that contains either today's or tomorrow's date, and mail all matched lines to you. The command will recognize dates in any of the following formats:

Sep 5

September 5

9/5

If you want to check the file yourself, you can execute the **calendar** command manually from the shell prompt, as shown here:

```
$ calendar
Sep 5      Monday at 9:30      Staff meeting
Sep 6      Tuesday at 2:00     Report on sales due
$ _
```

Basic Electronic Mail

With the **mail** command, you can send electronic mail to any user on your system, including yourself. The **mail** command is similar to the **write** command:

```
$ mail paul
Can you bring me the final chapters.  We have
to submit them this Friday.
CTRL D [not displayed]
$ _
```

In the preceding example, you typed the message after entering the **mail** command. You can also type the message first, store it in a file, then read from that file with the **mail** command. For example, suppose you have already stored the preceding message in a file called **chapters**. Then you can send the message to Paul with a command line like this:

```
$ mail paul < chapters
$ _
```

If necessary, you can also send your message to several users at the same time:

```
$ mail ann bill carl dana
We're trying to schedule the department
meeting on Thursday.  Let me know if you
can make it at 9:30.
CTRL D
$ _
```

Unlike **write** messages, **mail** messages don't reach their destinations immediately. Each recipient will learn about a message only after the next time the recipient logs in, as described below.

Whenever someone else sends you electronic mail, the system stores the message in a file named after your login name in directory **/usr/mail**. (For example, if your login name is **don**, your mail will be stored in **/usr/mail/ don**.) The next time you log in, the following message will appear on your screen:

```
You have mail
```

To see what has arrived since the last time you logged in, enter the **mail** command without arguments. The message sent to you most recently will be displayed on your screen, followed by a question mark (?). You can respond by typing one of the following **mail** commands (which can vary from one installation to another):

Command	Meaning
* (or ?)	List all **mail** commands
p	Redisplay (print) the current message
s [*file*]	Save the current message with header in *file* (save in **mbox** if no filename is given)
w [*file*]	Save the current message without header in *file* (save in **mbox** if no filename is given)
m *user*	Forward the current message to user
d	Delete the current message
Enter	Display (print) the next message
! *command*	Execute UNIX *command* without leaving **mail**
x	Exit **mail**, leaving all messages intact
q	Quit **mail**, leaving only unexamined messages

Every time you do something with the current message, the next message is displayed. Here is an example of displaying several messages and taking action on them:

```
$ mail
From penny Wed Nov 18 16:41:39 1990
I don't have the Burns report ready yet.
Ted and I should have it by Friday.
? s burns.rpt
From pat Wed Nov 18 13:04:28 1990
We have to have the Burns report by
Thursday.  Make sure it's ready.
? m penny
From rinnie Wed Nov 18 11:45:26 1990
I think you want to buy a fine new
300 baud modem.  I'm only asking $300,
one dollar per baud.  A real bargain!
? d
From henry Wed Nov 18 10:18:58 1990
Can you make it for racquetball Friday
afternoon at 12:30?
? q
$ mail henry
That sounds good.  I'll be there at 12:30.
CTRL D
$ _
```

In this sequence of messages, you saved the first message in **burns.rpt**. Then you forwarded the next message to Penny for her response. You deleted the third message and displayed the fourth. Finally, you quit **mail** to return to the shell prompt. Since you used the **q** command, the messages you looked at will be removed. After quitting **mail**, you sent a message of your own to Henry.

To view your messages in the order they were sent (that is, in reverse order), use the **−r** option with the **mail** command, as shown in the following example:

```
$ mail −r
From henry Wed Nov 18 10:18:58 1990
Can you make it for racquetball Friday
afternoon at 12:30?
? Enter
From rinnie Wed Nov 18 11:45:26 1990
I think you want to buy a fine new
300 baud modem.  I'm only asking $300,
one dollar per baud.  A real bargain!
? d
From pat Wed Nov 18 13:04:28 1990
We have to have the Burns report by
```

```
Thursday.   Make sure it's ready.
? m penny
From penny Wed Nov 18 16:41:39 1990
I don't have the Burns report ready yet.
Ted and I should have it by Friday.
? s burns.rpt
? q
```

Unless you request otherwise, your mail is stored in a file named after your login name in **/usr/mail**. For example, if your login name is **don**, your mail is stored in **/usr/mail/don**. To have your mail stored in your home directory, you can use the **−f** option with the **mail** command. If you don't provide a name, the name **mbox** will be used; otherwise, your name will be used. Here are some examples:

```
$ mail -f            Store mail in /usr/mail/mbox


$ mail -f hold       Store mail in /usr/mail/hold


$ mail -f store      Store mail in /usr/mail/store
```

Using the Extended Mail Facility

The Berkeley **mail** command, which is an enhanced version of the original **mail** command, is known as **mailx** in UNIX System V. If **mailx** is available on your system, you can use **mailx** instead of **mail**. One obvious difference is that **mailx** gives you a "Subject" prompt right after you enter the command line. An example of sending a message with **mailx** is as follows:

```
$ mailx ann bill carl dana
Subject: Department Meeting
We're trying to schedule the department
meeting on Thursday.  Let me know if you
can make it at 9:30.
CTRL D
$ _
```

One of the enhancements of **mailx** makes it possible for you to leave your message temporarily to take care of another task, and then return to entering your message. For example, suppose you have started typing your message when you remember that you left the names of Emma and Fred from your list of addressees. You can **escape** to add the two names with a command like this:

```
~t emma fred
```

Each of the **mailx** escape commands is constructed from a tilde (~) and another character. Here is a list of some of the other escape commands:

Command	Function
~?	Display all the escape commands
~t *user(s)*	Add names of user(s) to the "To" list
~c *user(s)*	Add names of user(s) to the "Copy" list
~s *title*	Enter a subject title
~h	Display prompts for "To," "Copy," and "Subject"
~v	Edit your message with the **vi** text editor
~r *file*	Read text into your message from *file*
~w *file*	Write your message to *file*
~p	Display (print) your message
~f *number(s)*	Read in other messages by number
~m *number(s)*	Read in other messages by number, indented to the first tab stop
~! *command*	Run a UNIX command, then return to **mailx**
~¦ *command*	Pipe the message to a UNIX command, replace the current message with the output, and return to **mailx**
~.	End your message
~A	Sign off, using **mailx** variable **Sign**
~a	Sign off, using alternate **mailx** variable **sign**
~x	Exit **mailx** and discard your message
~q	Quit **mailx** and save message in file **dead.letter**

To look at any mail that other users may have sent you, enter **mailx** by itself on a command line. You will see a one-line summary, called a **header**, for each message. At the beginning of each header you will find a sequence number (by which you can refer to the message) and one of the following codes:

```
N    New
R    Read
U    Unread
```

After the date and time, **mailx** gives you the size of the message in lines and characters. For example, **3/142** means three lines/142 characters. A pointer > indicates the current message, while a question mark (?) prompts you for a response, as shown in this example:

```
$ mailx
"/usr/mail/don": 6 messages 3 new 1 read 2 unread
  U  1 peter    Wed Jan 24 09:12    3/142     Weekly report
  R  2 terry    Wed Jan 24 10:03    5/317     Lunch meeting
  U  3 elaine   Wed Jan 24 11:38   10/736
  N  4 dwg      Wed Jan 24 14:27    4/228     Lost watch
  N  5 leslie   Wed Jan 24 17:05   18/1388
 >N  6 abdul    Thu Jan 25 08:44    6/467     Videotape
  ? _
```

To respond to a message, you can use any of the commands shown in the partial list below. In each instance, the full name is shown, but you can enter an abbreviated version of each command. As the brackets indicate, a message *list* is always optional. (More information about message lists follows.)

Command	Function
?	List **mailx** commands with explanations
=	Display the current message number
list	List **mailx** commands without explanations (**l**)
headers [*list*]	Display the page of headers indicated (**h**)
z	Scroll forward through the header list
z −	Scroll back through the header list
from [*list*]	Give header summary for messages (**f**)
top [*list*]	Display the first five lines of the messages selected (**to**)
next [*number*]	Display the next matching message (**n**)
print [*list*]	Display matching message(s) on the screen (**p**)
type [*list*]	Same as **print** (**t**)
Type [*list*]	Same as print (**T**)
hold [*list*]	Hold messages in **mbox** (**ho**)
preserve [*list*]	Same as **hold** (**pre**)
save [*list*] *file*	Save message(s) in *file* (s)
delete [*list*]	Delete message(s) (**d**)
undelete [*list*]	Restore message(s) deleted during current session (**u**)
edit [*list*]	Edit message(s) with default editor **ed** (**e**)
Reply [*list*]	Reply to sender only (**R**)
reply [*list*]	Reply to sender as well as other recipients (**r**)
cd [*dir*]	Change to directory *dir* (home directory if no name is given)
! *command*	Execute a UNIX command and return to **mailx**
exit	Exit **mailx**: save messages in **mbox** (**ex**)
xit	Same as **exit** (**x**)
quit	Quit **mailx**: save only unread messages in **mbox** (**q**)

The default for *list* is the current message, but you can define the message *list* as any set of messages you choose. You can use any of these symbols to set up a custom message list:

Symbol	Meaning
.	The current message
^	The first undeleted message
$	The last message
*	All messages
n	Message number *n*, where *n* is a whole number
n–m	Messages *n* through *m*
:n	All new messages
:o	All old messages

Symbol	Meaning
:r	All read messages
:u	All unread messages
:d	All deleted messages
/text	All messages that include *text* on the "Subject" line
name	All messages from user *name*

Unless you request otherwise, your mail is stored in a file named after your login name in **/usr/mail**. Like its counterpart for **mail**, the **−f** option for **mailx** allows you to choose the name of the file where your mail is stored. If you don't provide a name, the name **mbox** will be used; otherwise, your name will be used. Here are some examples:

```
$ mailx -f              Store mail in /usr/mail/mbox

$ mailx -f hold         Store mail in /usr/mail/hold

$ mailx -f store        Store mail in /usr/mail/store
```

External Communication

You can reach out and touch someone in more than one way from a UNIX system. You can reach just about anyone with a modem and a phone number with the call up command **cu**. (Some systems use **tip** instead of **cu**.) You can also reach a large number of UNIX systems on a network using the UNIX-to-UNIX copy command **uucp**.

Calling Another System

The **cu** command allows you to dial out to any system, UNIX or non-UNIX, that can be reached by modem. All the receiving side needs is a telephone number and a serial port. With the appropriate permissions, you can dial into another UNIX system and log in like any other user. Programmers and technicians do this to test the functioning of UNIX systems. You can use **cu** to aid in setting up a **uucp** network.

There are several ways you can reach another system. The most obvious is direct dialing. Suppose another system's number is (213) 555-3600 and suppose both systems are running at 1200 bits per second. Then you could reach the other system with a command line like this:

```
$ cu -s1200 2135553600
```

What happens next depends on what kind of system you are dialing into. Suppose you have just dialed into another UNIX system and suppose you have already set up a login account on that system. Then the other system will present a login prompt, and the beginning of your session will look like this:

```
$ cu -s1200 2135553600


Connected
login: don
Password:


%  _
```

If you want to keep a record of your **cu** session, you can capture the entire session in a file on your own system. Just pipe the session through the **tee** command. Here is an example, in which the session is captured in file **session**:

```
$ cu -s1200 2135553600 ¦ tee session


Connected
login: don
Password:


%  _
```

Direct dialing is not the only method for **cu**, however. You can also reach other UNIX systems across the **uucp** network. Your system has a list of names of the other UNIX systems that you can reach on this network. The list is in a file called either **/usr/lib/uucp/L.sys** (before System V, Release 3) or **/usr/lib/ uucp/Systems** (after System V, Release 3). To view the list, use the **uuname** command:

```
$ uuname
nike
apollo
mercury
minerva
athena
...
$  _
```

You can use any name on this list with the **cu** command to reach another UNIX system. Here is an example:

```
$ cu apollo


Connected
login: don
Password:


% _
```

If the other system's modem or serial port is busy, you won't succeed in making a connection immediately, and the attempt will look like this:

```
$ cu apollo
Connect failed: No Device Available
$ _
```

If you try to use a name that is not found in your system's list of available systems, this is what will happen:

```
$ cu thor
Connect failed: Requested device/system name not known.
```

Once you've succeeded in making a connection and logging into another UNIX system, you can use any UNIX commands on the other system that you would use on your own. Actually, once you've established a connection with another UNIX system, you find yourself straddling the two systems. You can now run commands on either system—a feature that will probably surprise DOS users.

The following general-purpose command can be used to send a file to any other system (UNIX or non-UNIX). If the name of the file is **memo**, the command line will look like this:

```
% ~> memo
24 lines/1893 characters
% _
```

In the examples in this chapter, we'll assume that the Bourne shell is running on your own system and the C shell is running on the other system. This assumption will make it easier to see which system a particular command is running on. In real life, the same shell may be running on both systems and a session with **cu** may become very confusing.

When both sides are UNIX systems and you have the required permissions, you can use this command to send a file to the other system:

```
% ~%put memo
stty -echo;cat - > memo;stty echo
24 lines/1893 characters
% _
```

You can also copy a file from your working directory on the other system to your working directory on your own system. Here is an example:

```
% ~%take new
stty -echo;mesg n;echo '~>':new;echo '~>';mesg y;stty echo
~>:new
29 lines/2284 characters
% _
```

To run a command on the other system, you just enter the command in the usual way:

```
% date
Fri Sep 1 17:32:56 PST 1990
% _
```

To run a command on your own system, as if there were no connection to another system, type ~! in front of the command. Here is an example with the same command:

```
% ~!date
Fri Sep 1 17:33:09 PST 1990
% _
```

To run a command on your own system, but send the output to the other system, type ~$ in front of the command. Here is a command that can be used to send a file to any other system (UNIX or non-UNIX):

```
% ~$cat report
% _
```

To change directories on your own system, type ~%, not ~!, in front of the **cd** command, as in this example:

```
% ~%cd sales
% _
```

After you've completed the session with **cu**, you can log out of the other system and terminate the session with the ~. command, as shown in the following example:

```
% CTRL D
login: ~.
Disconnected.
$ _
```

The appearance of the Bourne shell prompt tells you that you are no longer connected to another system. (In a real **cu** session, it may not be so obvious.) On some systems, the ~. command may log you out and disconnect you all at once. But it's safer to log out and disconnect in two steps, as shown in the preceding example.

UNIX-to-UNIX Communication

In the narrowest sense, **uucp** (UNIX-to-UNIX Copy) is one of many commands used for interacting between systems. But in a broader sense, uucp is used to encompass all the commands, as well as the network that supports them. If uucp is running on your system, you can use it to send electronic mail to other systems, exchange files with other systems, and execute commands on other systems.

For UNIX users, the uucp network is somewhat similar to The Source, CompuServe, and other commercial information services. A major difference is that uucp is integrated into the UNIX system. UNIX users with uucp can share disk and tape drives, laser printers, plotters, and other expensive resources.

We'll begin with electronic mail. If your system and neighboring systems are on the uucp network, you can exchange electronic mail with users on those systems. Suppose the systems shown in Figure 8-1 share a common uucp network.

If your system is nike, you can send mail directly to a user on mercury. Just include the name of the target system on the command line, followed by an exclamation mark (!), as shown here:

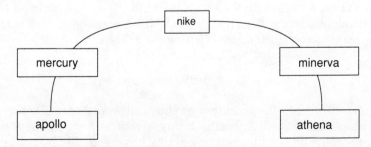

Figure 8-1. UNIX Systems in a Network

```
$ mail mercury!shelley
We'll be starting the softball game Saturday morning
at 9:30 in Willow Park.  We need you for short stop.
CTRL D
$ _
```

Intersystem electronic mail is slower than mail within your own system. It has to be queued for transmission, forwarded to its destination, and then discovered by the addressee. Chances are this will take at least a day. Once all these things happen, Shelley will see something like this:

```
From uucp Wed Mar 9 16:49 PDT 1990
>From don Tue Mar 8 10:23 PDT 1990 remote from nike
Status: R
We'll be starting the softball game Saturday morning
at 9:30 in Willow Park.  We need you for short stop.
```

Having received this message, Shelley can reply with a command line like this:

```
$ mail nike!don
Thanks for the reminder.  I'll be glad to get out
there and help beat the Coyotes.
CTRL D
$ _
```

In the previous example, the two systems were directly connected on the network. For the next example, we'll consider two systems that aren't directly connected. The *topology* of the network won't allow Don to send mail directly to Peter on system apollo. But he can route it through mercury, as shown in this example:

```
$ mail mercury!apollo!peter
I think we can get Shelley to play short stop on
Saturday.  Can you play center field?
CTRL D
$ _
```

Those who are closely associated with UNIX tend to prefer uucp addresses to telephone numbers. If you read UNIX magazines or look at UNIX bulletins, you are sure to come across listings like this:

```
John K. Unix
ucb!fremont!jku
```

A listing like the previous one above allows other readers or users to route a message or reply through the uucp network to the person named. If more than one route is possible, the choices will be surrounded by braces, as illustrated by the following address path:

```
{ucb,sun}!fremont!jku        ⎧ucb!fremont!jku
                             ⎨
                             ⎩sun!fremont!jku
```

The address path on the left is equivalent to the two on the right. When you send your message, you can use either one.

The main purpose of the uucp network is to allow users on different systems to exchange files. To help maintain security, a directory on each system called **/usr/spool/uucppublic** is usually designated for all file exchanges with other systems. This means that you will probably have to follow these four steps when you want to send a file to someone on another system:

- Grant other users permission to read the file if necessary
- Copy the file from your working directory to the public directory with **cp**
- Change to the public directory with **cd**
- Copy the file to the other system with **uucp**

Here is an example of following the four steps listed above. In this example, Don on system nike will send a file called **test** to user Jeff on system minerva, which is connected directly to nike on the uucp network:

```
$ pwd
/usr/don/work
$ chmod o+r test
$ cp test /usr/spool/uucppublic
$ cd /usr/spool/uucppublic
$ uucp text minerva!/usr/spool/uucppublic
$ _
```

You can abbreviate the last command line in the sequence shown above by replacing **/usr/spool/uucppublic** with ~/:

```
$ uucp test minerva!~/
$ _
```

In the C shell, the exclamation mark (!) has a special meaning related to the history feature. Therefore, when you use this symbol for any other purpose, you have to escape it with a backslash (\), for example:

```
% uucp test minerva\!/usr/spool/uucppublic
% _
```

Since electronic mail across the **uucp** network takes so long to complete, you may want to receive a message from the system when your message arrives at the other system's public directory. The mail option (**−m**) can be included in your **uucp** command line to provide this service. Here is an example for the Bourne shell:

```
$ uucp -m test minerva!~/test
$ _
```

Like **cp**, **uucp** also allows wildcard characters to help you select filenames. For example, suppose you wanted to send three files called **memo.1**, **memo.2**, and **memo.3** to your colleague on the other system. The command line would look like this:

```
$ uucp memo.? minerva!~/
$ _
```

The third main purpose of **uucp** is to allow you to use the **uux** command to execute commands on another system. Suppose several systems are sharing a laser printer on system nike. Then a user on mercury can use the laser printer by routing printing requests to nike like this:

```
$ cat news ! uux - nike!lp
$ _
```

The **cat** command pipes file **news** on system mercury to **uux**. The **uux** command will execute the **lp** command on system nike, which will place the file in the printing queue and send the originator a message like this:

```
From uucp Mon Oct 3 10:24 PST 1990
>From uucp Mon Oct 3 16:47 PST 1990 remote from nike
Status: R

uuxqt cmd (lp) status (exit 0, signal 0)
```

The zeroes in the last line indicate that the printing command was carried out successfully.

UNIX Bulletin Board

An informal bulletin board called USENET (Users' Network) is available on the **uucp** network (along with ARPANET and several other networks). If USENET has been installed at your site, you can take advantage of its features. You can read and respond to notices that other users have posted, and you can post notices of your own.

Notices for USENET have been grouped by user interest into approximately 250 newsgroups, under seven categories. Each newsgroup focuses on some political issue, academic subject, or recreational activity. The seven categories for newsgroups are listed in Table 8-1.

Table 8-1. USENET Categories

Category	Description
comp	Computer science
misc	Miscellaneous
news	Network news and users
rec	Recreational activities
sci	Natural sciences
soc	Social topics
talk	Discussion topics

To determine which newsgroups are available at your installation, use **more** or **pg** to list the contents of file **/usr/lib/news/newsgroups**:

```
$ more /usr/lib/news/newsgroups
```

ca.general	Of general interest to readers in California only
ca.driving	California freeways and backroads
ca.earthquakes	What's shakin' in California
ca.environment	Environmental concerns in California
ca.news	USENET status and usage in California
ca.news.group	Existing or proposed newsgroups for "ca" distribution
ca.politics	Political topics of interest to California readers only
ca.test	Tests of "ca" distribution articles
ca.unix	Unix discussion/help
ca.wanted	For Sale/Wanted postings throughout California
junk	Articles that we have no newsgroups for
comp.ai	Artificial intelligence discussions
comp.ai.digest	Artificial Intelligence discussions. (Moderated)

```
. . .
$ _
```

If you live in the Midwest, you won't find any of the California newsgroups. But you will find others relevant to your area. There are newsgroups for many states, all beginning with the two-letter postal abbreviations. Other geographic prefixes include usa (United States), can (Canada), na (North America), and so on.

Once you've looked at the list for your installation, if you find anything that interests you, can select the newsgroups you want to look at. (In USENET terminology, a list of newsgroups is called a *subscription list*, and you show your interest in a newsgroup by *subscribing* to it.) On USENET, as on most bulletin boards, commercial notices are not welcome.

Reading the Bulletin Board

Reading the bulletin board is a lot like going through your electronic mail for the day. You enter one of three commands to begin (**readnews**, **rn**, or **vnews**), depending on which command is used at your installation. In this chapter, we can't cover all three, so we'll pick **readnews** for the examples shown. The first notice appears, and you select one of a number of responses. (These responses vary from one command to the next.) This is how you would begin a session:

```
$ readnews
```

To review your subscription list, include the −**s** option, as shown here:

```
$ readnews -s
```

To display only those notices that relate to certain newsgroups (say **usa.unix** and **comp.ai.edu**), use the −**n** option to identify them:

```
$ readnews -n usa.unix comp.ai.edu
```

While you're looking at the notices on the bulletin board, you can use the following **readnews** commands:

Command	Function
?	Help
N	Go to the next newsgroup
U	Unsubscribe from the current newsgroup
b	Back up to the previous notice in the current newsgroup
−	Skip back to the previous notice
+	Skip to the next notice
e	Erase all memory of having read the current notice
s *file*	Save the current notice in *file*
r	Reply to the originator of a notice
f	Post a follow-up to a notice
Del	Discard the rest of a notice
x	Exit **readnews**

The commands will be different if your system uses **rn** or **vnews**.

Posting Your Own Notices

To comment on someone else's notice, always use the follow-up option **f** of the **readnews** command. Then your comment will be automatically linked to the earlier notice, and other users will know that the two are related.

To post an original notice, not directly related to another notice, use the **postnews** command (or **Pnews** if you are running **rn**). Begin by entering the **postnews** command:

```
$ postnews
Is this message in response to some other message? n
```

Your answer to the preceding question should always be no. If your answer is yes, then you are using the wrong command. As noted, you should be using the **postnews** command with the follow-up option **f**. Assuming your answer is no, the next two prompts will ask you for a subject and keywords. Make your subject as specific and narrow as you possibly can:

```
Subject: Looking for a tennis partner in Florida
Keywords: tennis sports outdoors
```

Next, you will have to enter the names of any newsgroups that pertain to your notice. If you aren't sure, you can press **?** for a list. Enter as many newsgroups as necessary; then press Enter on a prompt line after the last entry. Here is an example with just one newsgroup:

```
Newsgroups (enter one at a time, end with a blank line):

For a list of newsgroups, type ?
> rec.tennis
>
```

Then you will be prompted for geographic distribution. Again, always try to restrict the distribution to the smallest area you can. There is no point in advertising your private little notice all over the world. The default is usually your own state or province.

```
Distribution (default='fl', '?' for help): fl
```

After you've answered all the preliminary questions, the editor will start up and you can enter your actual notice. Type the notice the way you want it to appear on the bulletin board, and then save it with the **s** *file* command. At this point, the following messages will appear on the screen, indicating completion:

```
Posting article ...
Article posted successfully.
A copy has been saved in /usr/don/author_copy
```

If you post many notices, you may want to prepare a signature file, which contains your name, address, phone number, and **uucp** address. Both **postnews** and **Pnews** support a signature file called **.signature**, which is automatically appended to any notice that you post, for example:

```
$ cat .signature
James B. Heller (415) 555-3232
1800 Middlefield Way
Mountain View, CA 94040
sun!univax!heller
```

Preparing to Use the Bulletin Board

Until you set up your own subscription list, USENET will assign you a default list, which will include various general newsgroups. Once you become familiar with the bulletin board, you will probably want to construct your own subscription list. To do this, store the names of the newsgroups you want in your home directory in a file called **.newsrc**. You have to use this name; no other name is allowed.

Suppose you decide to subscribe to the following newsgroups: news.misc, comp.ai, rec.birds, rec.tennis, rec.chess, ca.news, and ca.driving. Then enter these names on the "options" line of **.newsrc**, separated by commas. Either create a new file or change the existing file. Here is how this example should look when completed:

```
$ cat .newsrc
options -n news.misc,comp.ai,rec.birds,rec.tennis,rec.chess,
 ca.news,ca.driving
$ _
```

If your list fills more than one line, start each new line with a blank space in the first column. Each time you begin a session with **readnews**, you will see the notices displayed by newsgroup in the order you specify in **.newsrc**.

Your entries in **.newsrc** can include wildcards to minimize typing. You can use **all** to select all subordinate newsgroups under a larger group or ! to exclude newsgroups. Type ! in front of the name; type **all** after a name. For example, to include everything related to California, but exclude everything related to computer science, enter your "options" line like this:

```
$ cat .newsrc
options -n ca.all !comp.all
$ _
```

## CHAPTER 9

BATCH FILES AND INITIALIZATION FILES

Introduction _____

If you have been using DOS for any length of time, then you are probably familiar with *batch files*. You store a sequence of commands in order in a batch file; then you execute the file like a command, and the commands are executed in the same order. It's as if you had entered each of the commands at the DOS prompt one at a time.

The UNIX counterpart of a batch file is a *shell program* (or *shell file* or *shell script*). You can place UNIX commands in a shell script, store them in a file, and then execute the file as if it were a command. Although the newer releases of DOS include many new features, UNIX shell scripts support many more programming features.

In the rest of this section, we'll construct a simple example, first in DOS, then in UNIX, and compare the two. Then, in the next section, we'll enlarge and expand the UNIX example, adding new functions one by one. In the last section of this chapter, we'll discuss initialization files in both systems, concluding with a closer look at the initialization files for the Bourne and C shells.

DOS Example

We'll begin with a very simple, very elementary example of a DOS batch file. Suppose you want to be able to display the date, time, and name and contents of the current directory. You could begin by entering the DATE, TIME, and DIR commands into a file, as shown below. In DOS, as you are probably aware, every batch file must have the extention **.BAT**. For this batch file, we'll use the name **DTDIR.BAT** (short for DATE/TIME/DIR):

```
C:\> COPY CON DTDIR.BAT
DATE
TIME
```

135

```
DIR
CTRL Z
C:\> _
```

Since this file has an extension of **.BAT**, it is ready to execute as soon as you've stored it. Just enter the basename (**DTDIR**) after the DOS prompt. Here is how the output will look:

```
C:\> DTDIR
Current date is Tue 9-17-1990
Enter new date (mm-dd-yy):
Current time is 10:28:38.47
Enter new time:

Volume in drive C is DEPARTMENT
Directory of C:\

COMMAND   COM    23791       12-30-85   12:00p
AUTOEXEC  BAT      256       11-08-88    2:54p
CONFIG    SYS      128        8-15-89    2:29p
VENTURA         <DIR>        11-10-88    8:30a
TYPESET         <DIR>        11-10-88    8:30a
SYSTEM          <DIR>        10-11-88    9:50a
PROGRAMS        <DIR>        10-11-88    9:51a
TEXT            <DIR>         9-01-88    6:07p
SCREEN          <DIR>         5-20-89   11:53a
TEMP            <DIR>         5-31-89   10:04a
         10 File(s)   10846208 bytes free
C:\>
```

In DOS, as long as you've set up your prompt properly, you don't have to include a separate command to display the name of the current directory. The three DOS commands included in **DTDIR.BAT** take care of all the functions required.

UNIX Example

Now we'll create an analogous file in UNIX, a shell script called **see.dir**. In this file we'll include three commands: **date**, **pwd**, and **ls −l**. Here is how you could enter the commands:

```
$ cat > see.dir
date
pwd
ls -l
CTRL D
$ _
```

You can begin to see a few differences already. The UNIX shell script can have any name you choose, and you use CTRL D to terminate text entry. Also, you have to include a command to display the name of the current directory. Finally, you have to make this file executable before you can start using it. Here is how you could do this:

```
$ chmod u+x see.dir
$ _
```

After you've run the command shown above, you can begin executing **see.dir** as if it were another UNIX command. The output will look something like this:

```
$ cd ../work
$ see.dir
Mon Jan 15 10:34:19 PST 1990
/usr/don/work
total 12
-rwxr----- 1 don   6782  Feb  3  10:54  addendum
drwx--x--- 1 don    367  Mar 15  08:37  balance
-rw-r--r-- 2 don   9285  Apr 22  15:21  call-125
drwx------ 1 don    294  Jan 18  11:46  deadline
-rwxrw---- 1 don   8349  Dec 17  08:59  end+odd
-rw-rw-rw- 5 don   7956  May 24  10:03  first
$ _
```

That takes care of it. The **see.dir** file displays the date, time, and name and contents of the current directory. This isn't a realistic shell script, but it does illustrate the differences between executable files in DOS and executable files in UNIX.

A Comparison

Before going on to the next section, let's review the similarities and differences between DOS and UNIX executable files.

DOS	UNIX
1. Creating the file: Use **COPY CON** or the ASCII output feature of your word processor.	Use **cat**, **ed**, or **vi**. Any of these will create standard files.
2. Terminating text entry: Use CTRL Z for **COPY CON**.	Use CTRL D for **cat**.
3. Making the file executable: Make sure the name of the file includes the extension **.BAT**.	Use the **chmod** command to make the file executable. The file can have any name you choose.

Expanding the UNIX Example

Now that you've seen the differences between DOS batch files and UNIX shell scripts, we'll examine UNIX shell scripts in greater detail. Because DOS has borrowed heavily from UNIX in recent releases, many of the features we'll look at in this section may also be found in DOS.

Allowing a Name on the Command Line

Let's add another command to our UNIX batch file that will allow us to change to the other directory before looking at its directory. We want to include the **cd** command in the shell script, but we don't want to give the name of the target directory right in the file. We want to be able to give the name of the target directory when we execute the shell script. Why? Suppose we include the following line in the shell script:

```
cd letters
```

Then we can use this shell script to change only to one directory (letters), and we would need a different shell script for each directory we wanted to change to. This won't work at all. The way to solve this problem is to use a variable in place of an actual directory name.

The shell variables that replace the arguments on a command line are called *positional parameters*. The name of each positional parameter includes a dollar sign ($) and a number to give its position on the command line. On each command line, $0 stands for the command name, $1 stands for the first argument, $2 stands for the second argument, $3 stands for the third, and so on. Here are some examples:

```
     $0        $1              $2
$ cp sample.doc sample.copy

     $0    $1       $2       $3        $4
$ mv memo.1 memo.2 memo.3 ../memos
```

If you've written many DOS batch files, note that in DOS you use a percent sign (%) instead of a dollar sign ($) and call them *replaceable parameters*. In DOS, the notation would be %0, %1, %2, %3, and so on. Also, the zero parameter %0 includes the name of the disk drive and directory path.

The **cd** command has only one argument, the target directory. So you need only two positional parameters:

```
     $0    $1
$ cd letters
```

To leave the target directory open for later substitution, include this line in your shell script:

```
cd $1
```

Here is another shell script that is identical to the previous shell script, with the addition of the line shown above:

```
$ cat > get.dir
cd $1              Change to the directory named
date               Display the date and time
pwd                Display the name of the directory
ls -l              List the contents of the directory
CTRL D
$ chmod u+x get.dir  Make get.dir executable
$ _
```

This shell script is now ready to use. There is one major difference, however, between **get.dir** and **see.dir**. When you use **get.dir**, you have to include a directory name. Here is an example of using **get.dir**:

```
$ pwd
/usr/don/letters
$ get.dir ../work
Fri Jun 29 15:03:37 PST 1990
/usr/don/work
total 12
-rwxr------ 1 don   6782  Feb  3 10:54 addendum
drwx--x--- 1 don    367  Mar 15 08:37 balance
-rw-r--r-- 2 don   9285  Apr 22 15:21 call-125
drwx------ 1 don    294  Jan 18 11:46 deadline
-rwxrw---- 1 don   8349  Dec 17 08:59 end+odd
-rw-rw-rw- 5 don   7956  May 24 10:03 first
$ _
```

The second line that follows the **get.dir** command (as well as the directory listing) shows that you have changed to the desired directory.

Interacting with Your Script

The two shell scripts that we've constructed so far have run on their own. However, you can also set up a shell script that you can interact with while it is running. You can give your shell script prompts and allow it to accept input from you. Three shell features provide your shell script with these features:

- A shell command called **echo** that puts prompts on the screen
- A shell command called **read** that accepts input from the user
- Shell variables of the form **$name** for storing user input

We'll now incorporate these three features into our shell script to make it interactive. Let's begin with the **echo** command, which displays text on the screen. Here is a simple example:

```
$ echo Test
Test
$ _
```

In the example above, we display only one word. But **echo** allows you to display more words and begin a new line if necessary. You can use the following two codes with **echo** to obtain the results indicated:

\c   Stay on the same line after displaying text

\n   Begin a new line after displaying text

The **\c** code is appropriate for prompts, allowing you to enter your response on the same line. The **\n** code is more suitable for messages, moving the cursor to the following line. When you use either of these codes, you must enclose the text within double quotation marks. We'll include them in the next version of our shell script, first after a prompt, then after a message to the user. This shell script will be called **goto.dir**:

```
$ cat > goto.dir
echo "Go to directory: \c"      Prompt for directory name
read dir                         Store name in dir
cd $dir                          Change to this directory
date                             Display the date and time
pwd                              Display the directory name
ls -l                            List the directory's contents
echo "You are now in $dir \n"    Display the name again
CTRL D
$ chmod u+x goto.dir             Make goto.dir executable
$ _
```

This third version of our shell script prompts the user for a directory name, stores the name in a variable, and uses this name in later commands. The directory name, stored in variable **$dir,** is used first by the **cd** command on the third line, then by the **echo** command on the seventh line. (Note that the variable name is preceded by a dollar sign when it is invoked, but not when it is assigned a value.) Here is how **goto.dir** works:

```
$ pwd
/usr/don/letters
$ goto.dir
Go to directory: _
```

At this point, the shell script prompts you for the name of the target directory. Once you enter a name, **goto.dir** continues, as shown here:

```
Go to directory: ../work
Fri Jun 29 15:03:37 PST 1990
/usr/don/work
total 12
-rwxr-----  1  don  6782  Feb  3  10:54  addendum
drwx--x---  1  don   367  Mar 15  08:37  balance
-rw-r--r--  2  don  9285  Apr 22  15:21  call-125
drwx------  1  don   294  Jan 18  11:46  deadline
-rwxrw----  1  don  8349  Dec 17  08:59  end+odd
-rw-rw-rw-  5  don  7956  May 24  10:03  first
You are now in directory: /usr/don/work
$ _
```

The results of **goto.dir** are similar to the results of **get.dir**. The main difference is that **goto.dir** prompts you for the name of the target directory, as noted previously. The message on the last line obtains the directory name shown from shell variable **$dir**. Although it isn't really very useful, this shell prompt illustrates many of the fundamental features of shell scripts.

Another Shell Script

Now we'll construct another shell script for practice. The purpose of this exercise is to help remedy one of the most frequent complaints about UNIX commands: "Their names are too illogical and they are too difficult to use." For example, if you wanted to change a file's name from **obscure** to **clear**, you would have to enter this command line:

```
$ mv obscure clear
$ _
```

The name of the command, **mv**, suggests that you are "moving" the file, rather than "renaming" it. For many users, it would be more convenient and less confusing to go through a sequence like the following:

```
$ rename
Name of file: obscure
Change name to: clear
Filename obscure changed to clear
$ _
```

Here is a shell script that will generate the friendly dialogue shown above:

```
$ cat rename
echo " Name of file: \c"
read before
echo " Change name to: \c"
```

```
read after
mv $before $after
echo " Filename $before changed to $after \n"
$ _
```

The preceding example provides a review of the **echo** and **read** commands and shell variables.

Skipping Positional Parameters

In a UNIX shell script, you can skip a positional parameter (or a sequence of parameters) and begin reading at the next one if necessary. The **shift** command instructs the shell to shift all positional parameters to the left, in effect skipping the first parameter and causing the second to be read as the first, the third to be read as the second, and so on.

Initialization Files

Initialization files provide an operating system with a set of operational parameters. In DOS, the primary initialization file is a batch file with a special name. In UNIX, the initialization files are just files with special names.

DOS Initialization Files

In DOS, one batch file plays a unique role in the operation of your system. Each time you boot your system, a special batch file called **AUTOEXEC.BAT** is automatically executed. You can use this file to set up pathnames for your commands, display the date and time, check your hard disk with **CHKDSK**, and run any other commands you wish. Here is an example of a typical **AUTOEXEC.BAT** file:

```
C:\> TYPE AUTOEXEC.BAT
ECHO OFF
CLS
VER
PROMPT=$P$G
PATH C:\VENTURA;C:\WP50;C:\MISC
DATE
TIME
CHKDSK C:
DIR
C:\> _
```

Without going into a lot of detail, the **AUTOEXEC.BAT** file clears the screen, displays the version number of DOS, sets up your DOS prompt to display your current directory, identifies the directories where your commands are stored, displays the date and time, checks your hard disk for you, and displays the contents of your root directory. The exact contents of this file may vary considerably from one system to another.

Another file used by DOS when you boot your system is **CONFIG.SYS**, the system configuration file. This file is used mainly to identify hardware that you have added to your system, set the maximum number of system buffers, and set the number of files that may be open at any given time. Here is an example:

```
C:\> TYPE CONFIG.SYS
DEVICE =\SYS\DOS\DRIVER.SYS /B:1
BUFFERS = 20
FILES = 30
C:\> _
```

Again, without delving into the details, the file displayed above indicates that you are designating a 3.5-inch disk drive as drive B, providing for 20 buffers, and allowing 30 files.

UNIX Bourne Shell Initialization File

In UNIX, each system has one file called **rc** (short for "run commands") that initializes the system as a whole. In addition, each user has a separate start-up file in his or her own home directory. In the Bourne shell, this file is called **.profile**, and it contains its own set of shell variables. We'll discuss **.profile** here, and defer **rc** to a later chapter. In the following sample file, four shell variables are assigned:

```
$ cat .profile
HOME=/usr/don
PATH=/bin:/usr/bin:$HOME/bin
MAIL=/usr/spool/lmail/"basename $HOME'
TERM=vt100
export HOME PATH MAIL TERM
$ _
```

The four shell variables assigned in the example above are summarized in Table 9-1, and described in detail below.

Login Directory. Running **cd** without an argument is equivalent to running **cd $HOME**. This variable is used on subsequent lines in **.profile**. In each instance, substitute the assigned value (**/usr/don**) in place of **$HOME**. The *basename* modifier used on the third line specifies extracting **don** from the full pathname **/usr/don**.

Table 9-1. Basic Bourne Shell Variables

Variable	Definition
HOME	**Home Directory.** The directory you log into.
PATH	**Command Search Path.** The directories that contain your commands.
MAIL	**Mail File.** The file that contains your incoming mail.
TERM	**Terminal Type.** Your terminal type.

Command Search Path. This variable lists the directories that contain command files, with colons (:) separating the names. In the sample shown above, the following directories are named:

```
/bin
/usr/bin
/usr/don/bin
```

Mail File. The file that stores your incoming mail is identified above as **/usr/spool/mail/don**.

Terminal Type. The **TERM** variable stores the type of terminal you are using. The name assigned must be identified in the terminal information file for your system, which must be one of the following:

```
/etc/termcap
/etc/terminfo/*/*
```

The older one, **/etc/termcap** is a single file, but **/etc/terminfo** is a directory that contains many files. You need to identify your terminal only for full-screen programs like **vi**.

Exporting Environmental Variables. The last line in the sample file *exports* the four environmental variables. That is, the settings for these variables now apply to all commands that you execute.

You usually set environmental variables in your set-up file. But it's also possible to set them from the command line. Here is an example of changing your terminal type:

```
$ TERM=tv950
$ export TERM
$ _
```

In the Bourne shell, it takes one command to assign a value to shell variable TERM and one to export the variable.

Additional variables that you can use in **.profile** are shown in Table 9-2.

Table 9-2. Other Bourne Shell Variables

Variable	Definition
CDPATH	Search path for the **cd** command, allowing you to use a relative pathname after **cd**.
MAILCHECK	Interval, in seconds, allowed for checking for the arrival of new mail. The default is 600 seconds.
MAILPATH	Like MAIL, except that you can list a series of files, separated by colons (:).
PS1	Primary prompt. The default is $.
PS2	Secondary prompt, used for commands that continue beyond one line. The default is >.
IFS	Internal field separator, which indicates where words end on a command line. Defaults are blank spaces, tab stops, and new lines.
SHACCT	Keep an accounting record in the file indicated of the execution of shell procedures.
SHELL	Check for running of the restricted shell (**rsh**). The **rsh** command is run any time an **r** appears in the assigned value of SHELL.

UNIX C Shell Initialization Files

The two initialization files for users of the C shell are discussed in Chapter 11, "Additional Control," which is devoted to the C shell. These files are closely related to other topics discussed in Chapter 11.

## CHAPTER 10

CONTROLLING YOUR SYSTEM

In the previous chapter, you learned how to use DOS batch files and UNIX shell scripts to execute a simple sequence of commands as one command. In this chapter, we'll explore methods for putting more selectivity into these useful files. The features of the shell allow you to carry out more sophisticated tasks and build decision-making into your shell scripts.

Because recent releases of DOS have borrowed heavily from UNIX, you can now use many of the same features in DOS batch files. (You can also use a lot of the same esoteric notation because DOS has borrowed that, too.)

Another Look At Redirection

Redirection is one of the features that DOS has borrowed from UNIX. As you have learned by now, you can use one of three types of notation to perform redirection.

Ordinary Redirection

You can redirect command input from a file, as shown in the following example. Here, the **mail** command sends the text that is already stored in file **note** rather than the text that you type from your keyboard. The input is redirected from file **note**.

```
$ mail jerry < note
$ _
```

You redirect command output to a file, as shown in the next example. Here, the line of text you type is stored in file **test** rather than just displayed on the screen. The redirection is to file **test**.

```
$ cat > test
This is a test.
CTRL D
$ _
```

Finally, you can append command output to a file, as shown in the final example. This example is just like the previous one, except that the text you type is appended to the text that is already stored in the file. (If the file doesn't exist when you start, then > is the same as > >.)

```
$ cat >> test
Here is a second line.
CTRL D
$ _
```

File Descriptors

Whenever you enter a UNIX command, the system opens three files, each associated with a number called a **file descriptor**. The three file descriptors are as follows:

- 0: standard input
- 1: standard output
- 2: diagnostic output

For each of these, your terminal is the default. The default standard input is from your keyboard; the default standard output and diagnostic output is to your screen.

You can redirect standard output or diagnostic output to different destinations by including file descriptors in your command lines. Just use the appropriate number with an ampersand (&) following the redirection symbol. Here is the notation:

- **1>&** Redirect standard output to the destination indicated
- **2>&** Redirect diagnostic output to the destination indicated

For example, to send the contents of file **test** to one file named **output** and any error message that may be issued to another file called **error**, you can construct your command line like this:

```
$ cat test 1>&output 2>&error
$ _
```

You don't necessarily have to separate your standard output from your error output. You can send both to the same file, **catch**, by using the following construction:

```
$ cat test 1>&catch 2>&1
$ _
```

In the previous example, the notation **2>&1** means, "Send any errors to the same destination to which standard output is being sent." In this example, the destination is file **catch**.

Using Variables

In UNIX, you can use your own abbreviations for longer names. Then, when you need to refer to the longer name, you can just type the abbreviation instead. For example, suppose you work frequently in a directory called **/usr/larry/electronics/stereo**. You can assign this long name to a shorter mnemonic like **hifi**, as shown here:

```
$ hifi=/usr/larry/electronics/stereo
$ _
```

Now you can use your abbreviation in your command lines. Just precede the name with a dollar sign ($) to identify it as a shell variable. Here is an example:

```
$ cd $hifi
$ pwd
/usr/larry/electronics/stereo
$ _
```

To the shell, it is as if you had typed the following on the first line above:

```
$ cd /usr/larry/electronics/stereo
$ _
```

Assigning More Than One Word

If the expression that you are assigning to an abbreviation is more than a single word, you have to enclose it within a pair of single quotation marks. In other words, use single quotes if it contains any of these:

- blank spaces
- tabs
- semicolons (;)
- newlines

For example, suppose you frequently format complex material that contains tables and equations. Each time you start a new job, you have to enter a command line like this:

```
$ mm -E -t -e -c -T4000a report ¦ lp
```

You can simplify your job by assigning an abbreviation like this:

```
$ start='mm -E -t -e -c -t4000a'
$ _
```

Then, the next time you have to start a formatting job, you can enter a command line like this:

```
$ $start report | lp
```

When the shell reads this command line, it determines from the dollar sign that **$start** is a shell variable. Then it replaces the string previously assigned, thereby expanding the command line into the following:

```
$ mm -E -t -e -c -T4000a report | lp
```

Use variables for any command lines that are difficult to type. In the previous example, we used a variable in place of a command line that contained many arguments. You could also use a variable for a command line that contained many strange symbols. This is a good way to neutralize some of the esoteric notation of UNIX.

Allowing Variable Substitution

You may want to substitute one shell variable within the assignment of another. To allow this, enclose the string being assigned between a pair of double quotation marks. In other words, use double quotes whenever it contains any of the following:

- Dollar signs ($)
- Single quotes (')
- Double quotes (")

Continuing with the previous example, suppose you do some printing on one printer for draft copies and some printing on another for final copies. The command lines could look like this:

Draft copies:

```
$ mm -E -t -e -c -T4000a report | lp
```

Final copies:

```
$ mm -E -t -e -Thp report | lp
```

The two command lines are identical, except for the text between −**e** and the name of the document, **report**. You could leave this to be assigned at the time you enter the command line, using another variable, like **P** for printer. Then you could redefine shell variable **start** as shown here:

```
$ start="mm -E -t -e $P"
$ _
```

In the assignment shown above, the double quotation marks allow you to include another shell variable within the string being assigned. When you're ready to perform actual printing, you can follow a sequence like the following:

```
$ P='-c -T4000a'
```

or

```
$ P=-Thp
```

then

```
$ $start report ¦ lp
```

Because of the double quotation marks in the assignment statement for **start** above, the shell reads the **$P** in the string as a shell variable and substitutes its value into the final command line. Here is a pictorial representation of what happens:

1. You enter the abbreviated command line:

```
$ $start report ¦ lp
```

2. The shell expands **$start**, substituting its value:

```
$ mm -E -t -e $P report ¦ lp
```

3. The shell expands **$P**, substituting its value:

```
$ mm -E -t -e -c -T4000a report ¦ lp
```

If you used single quotation marks in the assignment statement for **start**, step 3 above would not take place, and the final command line to be executed would be the one shown in step 2, which the shell could not execute. The shell would display an error message, and nothing would happen.

Substituting a Command's Output

Finally, you may want to take the output of a command and use it in a variable substitution. To allow this to happen, enclose the command's name within grave accent marks (` ` `). For example, suppose you want to keep track of the name of a directory while you work in another. Assign the name of the current directory to a variable while you are in that directory (with the help of the **pwd** command). Then you can return to that directory quickly and easily. Here is an example:

1. Move to the first directory:

```
$ cd /usr/janice/current/notes
$ _
```

2. Store the name of the first directory:

```
$ here=`pwd`
$ _
```

3. Move to a second directory:

```
$ cd /usr/david/patterns/results
$ _
```

4. Store the name of the second directory:

```
$ there=`pwd`
$ _
```

5. After working in the second directory for a while, move back to the first:

```
$ cd $here
$ _
```

6. After working in the first directory for a while, move back to the second again:

```
$ cd $there
$ _
```

You could switch back and forth between the two directories many times with these simple command lines. If you want to, you can use even shorter names for the shell variables. For example, suppose you have to work in three different directories. You can give them three simple names like these:

- d1   First directory
- d2   Second directory
- d3   Third directory

Then you can switch to the third directory by entering the following command line:

```
$ cd $d3
$ _
```

Controlling The Outcome

So far in this chapter, the emphasis has been on techniques you can use to perform everyday tasks. Now we'll shift the emphasis to UNIX shell scripts, which are analogous to DOS batch files. We'll look at various methods for executing a sequence of commands stored in a file.

By setting up alternative courses of action, you can construct shell scripts that allow decision-making. You can do this in DOS as well as in UNIX, but the notation is a little different in DOS.

Setting Up a Conditional Statement

You can set up conditional statements that allow the shell to check for something and then take a predefined action, depending on the result of the check. The syntax is based on common English usage. In everyday language, you make statements like the following:

1. "If it rains today, we'll have to stay home."
     or
2. "If it rains today, then we'll have to stay home."
3. "If she gets here by 3:00, we'll make it on time."
     or
4. "If she gets here by 3:00, then we'll make it on time."

Sentences 1–4 are examples of conditional statements. In English, the word *then* is optional. So sentences 1 and 2 are identical in meaning, and so are sentences 3 and 4. In batch files, DOS uses the convention illustrated by sentences 1 and 3; in shell scripts, UNIX uses the convention illustrated by sentences 2 and 4.

In UNIX, the condition is usually placed on one line and the action statement on another. Finally, each **if...then** statement is ended with the word **fi** (**if** spelled backwards). To allow testing, the shell also allows you to use the words **true** and **false**. Here is a simple example of a complete conditional statement:

```
$ cat T
if true
      then echo 'Display only if true'
fi
$ _
```

If you make shell script **T** executable and run it, you see the message displayed:

```
$ T
Display only if true
$ _
```

Here is a similar shell script, with **true** replaced by **false**:

```
$ cat F
if false
      then echo 'Display only if true'
fi
$ _
```

If you make this shell script executable and run it, you don't see any output:

```
$ F
$ _
```

Setting Up an Alternative Action

In the previous example, when the shell found the condition false, it skipped the only statement it found and there was no output. However, you can provide an alternative course of action for instances when the condition is false. The key word, which is also used in everyday language, is **else**. You could modify shell script **F** shown above to include a third clause, as shown here:

```
$ cat F
if false
      then echo 'Display only if true'
      else echo 'Display only if false'
fi
$ _
```

Now if you run shell script **F** again, you will see the new statement displayed, as shown here:

```
$ F
Display only if false
$ _
```

Making a Test

In a shell script, you have a number of ways of testing files, strings, and quantities. You often want to use the results of these tests in your conditional statements. You may want to know whether a given file exists or whether its name matches a name you are looking for. To indicate any of these tests, surround the expression within a pair of brackets. For example, to test whether ordinary file **sample** exists, type **[−f sample]**. (Before System V, the word **test** was used instead of brackets. For this example, you would type **test −f sample**.)

For example, if you are planning to copy files, you may want to check first to make sure the file doesn't already exist. Then, when you're sure that it doesn't, you can carry out the copy. Let's say you plan to copy a file. You want to call your shell script **copy**, and you want to use the following syntax to copy a file called **sample** to **sample_2**:

```
$ copy sample sample_2
File sample copied
$ _
```

Here's how you could use a test to copy the file safely. Again, the line numbers are not part of the shell script. They are used only to allow easy reference to the statements.

```
   $ cat copy
1. if [ -f $2 ]
2.      then echo 'File already exists'
3.      else cp $1 $2
4.          echo "File $1 copied"
5. fi
   $ _
```

Here is a brief description of each statement in the shell script shown above:

Line 1. Test to determine whether a file by this name (**$2**) already exists. This statement, when expanded by the shell, is **[−f sample_2]**.

Line 2. If it does exist, display the message, "File already exists."

Line 3. If it does not exist, copy the file to the target directory and . . .

Line 4. Display the message, "File **sample** copied."

Line 5. End of the conditional statement.

The −**f** symbol to test for the existence of a file isn't the only one available to you. You can use the notation [− d *name*] to test for the existence of a directory. All together, you can use any of five different symbols:

$$
\left[\left\{
\begin{array}{l}
\texttt{-r} \\
\texttt{-w} \\
\texttt{-f} \\
\texttt{-d} \\
\texttt{-s}
\end{array}
\right\} \textit{name}\, \right]
\quad
\begin{array}{l}
\text{Does the file exist and can it be read?} \\
\text{Does the file exist and can it be written to?} \\
\text{Does the file exist and is it ordinary?} \\
\text{Does the directory exist?} \\
\text{Is the file non-empty?}
\end{array}
$$

Working Through a List

Many tasks involve taking a list of items and performing some action on each item in the list. It could be a list of filenames or a list of directory names. The task could be to copy each file listed to a backup device. First, let's begin with a simpler task: displaying names on the screen. Here is the shell script:

```
$ cat show
1. list='Art Bea Charles Dana Evan'
2. for NAME in $list
3.      do echo $NAME
4.      done
5. echo 'THE END'
$ _
```

Here is an explanation of each step in **show**:

Line 1. Assign to shell variable **list** a set of five names. Because there are blank spaces between the names, we have to use single quotation marks.

Line 2. Using another variable called **NAME**, indicate that you want to step through each name in the list assigned in line 1.

Line 3. The **do** statement introduces the action to be performed. In this instance, it is simply to display the current name on the screen. Since there are five names in the list, the action will be repeated five times.

Line 4. The **done** statement is necessary to end the **do** statement. You could include an entire sequence of commands between **do** and **done**.

Line 5. Because this line follows the **done** statement, it is executed only once—after all names in the list have been displayed.

Assuming that you've made **show** executable, you can now run **show**, with the output shown:

```
$ show
Art
Bea
Charles
Dana
Evan
THE END
$ _
```

One way to use a **for** loop would be to move a group of files from one directory to another. In the example that follows, we'll create a shell script called **moveto** that moves all files in the current directory to a target directory named on the command line. Here is how the shell script would look:

```
$ cat moveto
1. list=`ls`
2. for FILE in $list
3.      do mv $FILE $1
4.      echo $FILE
5.      done
6. echo 'FILES MOVED'
$ _
```

Here is what each line in this shell script does:

Line 1. Assign to shell variable **list** the names of the files in the current directory. (You don't have to use the name **list**; you could use **files** or another name.)

Line 2. Set up a loop that will take each name in your list one at a time and feed it to the statement in line 3.

Line 3. Use the **mv** command to move each file to the target directory, here indicated by the notation **$1**.

Line 4. Display the name of the file just moved.

Line 5. End the **for** loop.

Line 6. Display a message at the end of the list.

Suppose you want to move all the files in the current directory (/**usr/andre/work**) to another directory called /**usr/andre/backup**. Then, once you've made **moveto** executable, you can enter the following on the command line. If the current directory contains five files called **memo.1**, **memo.2**, **memo.3**, **letter.1**, and **letter.2**, the output will be as shown below:

```
$ moveto ../backup
memo.1
memo.2
memo.3
letter.1
letter.2
FILES MOVED
$ _
```

Setting Up Menu Selections

You can build menu selections into your shell scripts with the **case** command. This command reads input from the keyboard and switches control to one of a series of separate choices. For each choice, you insert the appropriate commands. In a real-life example, each choice would include a long sequence of commands. In the simple example that follows, we'll merely display a message on the screen to indicate what the user has selected. We'll provide four regular choices, plus a catchall for incorrect entries. The four regular choices will be (1) select a directory, (2) edit a document, (3) format a document, and (4) end this session.

```
    $ cat doc.menu
 1. echo '                 DOCUMENT MENU\n\n'
 2. echo '1    Select a directory        D or d'
 3. echo '2    Edit a document           E or e'
 4. echo '3    Format a document         F or f'
 5. echo '4    Exit                      X or x'
 6. echo '    Enter the number or letter: \c'
 7. read choice
 8. case $choice in
 9.       1|D|d) echo 'Change to a new directory' ;;
10.       2|E|e) echo 'Prepare to begin editing' ;;
11.       3|F|f) echo 'Prepare to begin formatting' ;;
12.       4|X|x) echo 'This session is over' ;;
13.       *) echo 'Type D, E, F, or X' ;;
14. esac
    $ _
```

Lines 1–7 display the menu on the screen, offering the user four choices, with three alternative characters for each choice. On line 7, the user's input is stored in shell variable **choice**. Here is a description of each of the remaining lines:

Line 8. The **case** statement uses the character entered by the user, stored in variable **choice**, to switch to one of the four choices (line 9, 10, 11, or 12).

Line 9. This is the first of the four choices. It begins with the three characters the user can enter to make this choice (1, D, or d). After the right parenthesis, enter the commands to be executed, followed by a pair of semicolons (;;).

Line 10. This is the second choice, invoked with 2, E, or e.

Line 11. This is the third choice, invoked with 3, F, or f.

Line 12. This is the fourth choice, invoked with 4, X, or x.

Line 13. The asterisk (*) here indicates that this line is executed if the user enters any character other than one of the 12 already named. This is a prompt to enter one of those characters.

Line 14. An **esac** line (**case** spelled backward) is required to end the **case** command.

After you've made **doc.menu** executable, you can enter the command with results like these:

```
$ doc.menu
               DOCUMENT MENU
1      Select a directory      D or d
2      Edit a document         E or e
3      Format a document       F or f
4      Exit                    X or x
       Enter the number or letter: _
```

If you enter **D**, the following message will appear on the screen:

```
Change to a new directory
```

In a real-life menu, another prompt would appear now, requesting the name of the new directory. You would enter the name, the shell would move you to the directory, and the menu would return for another choice.

Putting It All Together

In one example in the previous section, we moved a group of files to another directory. The shell script was very basic, with no built-in safeguards. If we incorporate some of the testing from a little earlier in the section, we can construct a more sophisticated shell script that automatically does some checking for us before going to work. Then we can make the entire procedure a choice on a menu.

Incorporating Safeguards

We'll begin by inserting a test for each file to make sure that a file by the same name doesn't exist in the target directory. The test is on line 3 in the shell script shown below, with the new message on line 4. Here is the new shell script:

```
     $ cat moveto
1. list=`ls`
2. for FILE in $list
3.      do if [ -f $1/$FILE ]
4.          then echo 'File already exists'
5.          else mv $FILE $1; echo $FILE
6.      fi
7.      done
8. echo 'FILES MOVED'
   $ _
```

This new script combines two scripts developed earlier in this chapter, one for checking for existing files and one for moving files to another directory.

Placing the Procedure in a Menu

Next, we'll take the procedure for moving files to another directory and place it in a menu. In the example that follows, this procedure will be the third choice. We'll insert this procedure after the message for the third choice, moving files. Here is the new shell script:

```
     $ cat file.menu
1. echo '              FILE MENU\n\n'
2. echo '1   Copy files              C or c'
3. echo '2   Delete files            D or d'
4. echo '3   Move files              M or m'
5. echo '4   Exit                    X or x'
6. echo '    Enter the number or letter: \c'
7. read choice
8. case $choice in
9.      1|C|c) echo 'Prepare to copy files' ;;
10.     2|D|d) echo 'Prepare to delete files' ;;
11.     3|M|m) echo 'Prepare to move files' ;
12.          echo 'Enter name of target directory: \c'
13.          read $dir
14.          list=`ls`
15.          for FILE in $list
16.              do if [ -f $dir/$FILE ]
17.                  then echo 'File already exists'
18.                  else mv $FILE $dir; echo $FILE
19.              fi
20.              done
21.          echo 'FILES MOVED' ;;
```

```
22.      4¦X¦x) echo 'This session is over' ;;
23.      *) echo 'Type C, D, M, or X' ;;
24. esac
   $ _
```

Now we have combined three smaller shell scripts developed earlier in the chapter to produce a larger script. With this new script, when you select moving files (3, M, or m) from the menu, the shell executes lines 11–19. Lines 11–19 carry out the actual move, with checking included. Note that line 11 now ends with a single semicolon (;), the symbol for separating one UNIX command from another. The double semicolon (;;) is now at the end of line 19, where it indicates the end of the procedure. (Lines 12–19, of course, represent the shell script we just constructed in the previous subsection.)

We still don't have a complete script; we would have to fill in the procedures for copying and deleting files to have a complete script. But you have learned how you can construct a useful, easy-to-use script with only a few simple concepts to work with.

As an exercise, you may want to fill in the other two procedures yourself. Insert the procedure for copying files after line 9. Then insert the one for deleting files after line 10. In each instance, remember to move the pair of semicolons to the end of the procedure.

## CHAPTER 11

ADDITIONAL CONTROL

In the previous chapter, you learned how to control your system using the Bourne shell. In this chapter, you will learn how to provide additional control using the C shell. Acually, you will probably use one shell or the other, not both.

Initialization Files for the C Shell

As you learned in the previous chapter, the Bourne shell has only one initialization file. But the C shell has two: **.login** and **.cshrc**. The **.login** file is quite a bit like the Bourne shell's **.profile** file, but **.cshrc** is different. For the most part, **.cshrc** describes features found only in the C shell. When you log in, the C shell executes **.cshrc** before **.login**, but we'll discuss them in reverse order, beginning with the file that is more similar to the Bourne shell's initialization file.

The C Shell Login File

The C shell executes the **.login** file only when you log in. This file contains information relating to the basic functioning of your terminal. The statements stored in **.login** are similar to those stored in the Bourne shell's **.profile**, but the construction is a little different. Here is a very simple example in three lines:

```
% cat .login
1. stty erase "^H" kill "^A"
2. set path=(/bin /usr/bin $HOME/bin .)
3. setenv TERM tv950
%
```

Now we'll discuss each line by number.

Line 1. *Terminal settings.* The set terminal command, **stty**, assigns the erase key to CTRL H and the kill key to CTRL A. These are the key combinations that allow you to erase the previous keystroke and erase the command line. Note that the C shell uses quotation marks around the names of the control characters.

Line 2. *Command search path.* This line is similar to those used by the Bourne shell and DOS, but with small differences. Here, the list is surrounded by parentheses, but contains blank spaces instead of colons (:) as separators. In addition, the word *path* is preceded by the word *set* and neither word is capitalized. Once again, **$HOME** represents your home directory. So if your home directory is **/usr/ben**, the C shell will search the following directories for commands that you enter at the command line:

```
/bin
/usr/bin
/usr/ben/bin
```

Line 3. *Terminal assignment.* This line assigns the value "tv950" to variable TERM, allowing you to use programs, such as **vi**, that require full-screen processing. This value, which represents the TeleVideo 950, must be defined in your system's terminal database. That is, either **/etc/termcap** or **/usr/lib/terminfo/t/tv950** must contain a description for "tv950."

Note the difference between the C shell command on line 3 and the Bourne shell command. Actually, the Bourne shell requires two separate commands:

```
TERM=tv950
export TERM
```

However, the C shell does exactly the same thing with a single command, the set environment command:

```
setenv TERM tv950
```

The C Shell Run Command File

The C shell executes the **.cshrc** file each time the system creates a new C shell (that is, when you log in and any time you start a C shell script). The file is used to do three things, two of which relate to features unique to the C shell.

We'll define these features and then list the three functions of **.cshrc**. In the C shell, command lines are called **events**. A sequence of events stored for later reference is called a **history** list. Next, a custom command that you define for your own use is called an **alias**. Now that you are familiar with these terms, here are the three main functions of **.cshrc**:

- Set your shell prompt
- Set the length of your history list
- Define your aliases

Here is a simple example of a **.cshrc** file with numbered lines for easy reference:

```
% cat .cshrc
1. set prompt = "\!% "
2. set history = 12
3. alias ti        cd /usr/lib/terminfo/t
4. alias up        cd /usr/lib/uucppublic/pat
5. alias view      cd '\!*; ls -l | more'
6. alias vt        vi /usr/pat/admin/totals
%-
```

Line 1. *Your shell prompt.* The C shell not only allows you to set your own shell prompt, it also provides automatic line-numbering. This is a handy convenience that you should take advantage of. In line 1 above, we are requesting automatic numbering of command lines, followed by a percent sign and a blank space. Once you've activated this **.cshrc** file, your first shell prompt will look like this:

```
1% _
```

Line-numbering is particularly useful to the C shell's history mechanism, which you will learn about next.

Line 2. *Length of the history list.* Again, each command line that you enter for the C shell is called an event. The C shell stores a certain number of these events for later reference in its history list. In line 2 above, we are requesting a history list of 12 events. In other words, we are asking the C shell to save the 12 most recent command lines that we enter at the prompt. Since we asked for line-numbering on line 1 of **.cshrc**, it will be easy to identify events in the history list by number.

Each UNIX system allows a certain maximum number of events in each user's history list, often around 25 or so. Although the **.cshrc** file is the best place to set the length of the list, you can also set it on a command line, as shown here:

```
1% set history = 5
2% _
```

When you make this setting, you are telling the C shell to store only the five most recent events. If you want to take a look at the list, you can enter the **history** command alone, as shown here:

```
26% history
     21  cd
     22  cd MEMOS
     23  pwd
     24  ls -l
     25  vi memo.736
27% _
```

As you will learn in the next section, you can retrieve any event in your current history list and run it again. You can also make changes in the event before you run it the second time.

Line 3. *First alias*. This line allows you to enter **ti** in place of **cd /usr/lib/ terminfo/t** as a command line. In this instance, you save 20 keystrokes. With other aliases, you can save even more.

Line 4–6. *Three more aliases*. These lines define aliases **up**, **view**, and **vt**, which are similar to **ti**. We'll defer further discussion of aliases to later in this chapter.

Retrieving Events

The C shell allows you to retrieve any event in your current history list and rerun it. Considering the length of some of your command lines, this feature can be an enormous convenience. Once you've seen the history list, you can reexecute either the most recent event or any event by number.

Reexecuting an event involves typing at least one exclamation mark (!). If you want to use an exclamation mark for any other purpose, such as setting up automatic line-numbering, you have to use a backslash (\) to escape it. That's why you saw the notation \!% in the **.cshrd** file shown earlier in this chapter.

Reexecuting the Previous Event

Let's continue where we left off in the previous section. Suppose you've just displayed the history list, as shown here:

```
26% history
     21  cd
     22  cd MEMOS
     23  pwd
     24  ls -l
     25  vi memo.736
27% _
```

You can repeat this event by entering !! on command line 27, as shown below:

```
27% !!
history
        21  cd
        22  cd MEMOS
        23  pwd
        24  ls -l
        25  vi memo.736
28% _
```

When you reexecute an event in this way, the C shell displays the command line itself and then the output, as shown above.

Reexecuting Any Event

Now that we're on command line 28, the only event we can repeat with **!!** is number 27. Suppose we want to reexecute number 23. Then we can enter the following to display the name of the current directory again:

```
28% !23
pwd
/usr/dan/MEMOS
29% _
```

In the simple example shown above, you don't actually save any keystrokes. But if event number 23 were **cd /usr/lib/terminfo/t**, you would save 16 keystrokes.

Selecting Arguments _____

In Chapter 9, "Batch Files and Initialization Files," you saw how the Bourne shell identifies individual arguments on a command line with positional parameters. The C shell also uses positional parameters, as illustrated in the following example:

```
17% cp memo.1 memo.2 memo.3 ../plans
18% _
```

The command line shown above includes a command and four arguments, which are enumerated below:

```
$0    cp
$1    memo.1
$2    memo.2
$3    memo.3
$4    ../plans
```

Selecting Any Argument

While you are retrieving an event in your history list, you can select any argument by number. Just type a colon (:) and the number at the end of your command to retrieve the event. Suppose you want to use the third argument from event 17 in another command line. Then you can use the following command line:

```
19% cat !17:3
cat memo.3
ZELCO TIMERS
M E M O
FROM:     Jan Peters              DATE: May 12, 1990
TO:       All Managers
SUBJECT:  Missing Timecards
=============================================================
.
.
.
20% _
```

Command line 19 means, "Use the third argument from event 17 as the argument for the **cat** command on this line." The first number (17) identifies the event; the second number (3) identifies the argument to be extracted from that command line.

Next you will learn how to select arguments with other forms of the basic notation. To make it very easy to follow the discussion, we'll use the **echo** command shown below in all the examples. With this command, there will be no doubt which argument (or arguments) you are selecting. Here is the command line:

```
30% echo arg.1 arg.2 arg.3 arg.4 arg.5 arg.6
arg.1 arg.2 arg.3 arg.4 arg.5 arg.6
31% _
```

Selecting the First Argument

To select the first argument, you can use either a one (1) or a caret symbol (^). If you use a caret symbol, you can omit the colon (:). These two examples are equivalent:

```
31% echo !30:1            31% echo !30^
echo arg.1                echo arg.1
arg.1                     arg.1
32% _                     32% _
```

Selecting the Last Argument

To select the last argument, you can use either the number or a dollar sign ($). The dollar sign is much more convenient because you usually don't know exactly how many arguments there are on a command line. Again, if you use a dollar sign, you can omit the colon. Here are two equivalent examples:

```
32% echo !30:6          32% echo !30$
echo arg.6              echo arg.6
arg.6                   arg.6
33% _                   33% _
```

Selecting More Than One Argument

To select more than one argument at once, you can type a range of numbers, separated by a hyphen. For example, to select arguments 3, 4, and 5, you can use the following notation:

```
33% echo !30:3-5
echo arg.3 arg.4 arg.5
arg.3 arg.4 arg.5
34% _
```

Selecting All Arguments

To select every argument on the command line, you can use a wildcard character (*). Again, you can omit the colon, as shown here:

```
34% echo !30*
echo arg.1 arg.2 arg.3 arg.4 arg.5 arg.6
arg.1 arg.2 arg.3 arg.4 arg.5 arg.6
35% _
```

This notation is much more useful if you use a different command, as shown in the next example:

```
35% mv !30* ../backup
mv arg.1 arg.2 arg.3 arg.4 arg.5 arg.6 ../backup
36% _
```

Since we didn't use the **echo** command in the example above, you don't see the results as plainly. But you can check the two directories to see what has happened (the six files have been moved to directory **backup**).

Making Changes to a Command Line _____

You have already learned how to reexecute an event intact or with selected arguments. Now you will learn how to reexecute it with changes in it. The C shell provides several one-letter modifiers that you can type after the colon. We'll discuss three of them here.

Substituting Arguments

You may recall using **vi**'s substitute command **s** in Chapter 6, "Editing Text." The C shell's substitute modifier is very similar. For example, to change **a** to **A** in the first argument, you can append **s/a/A** to the basic command, as shown here:

```
31% !30:s/a/A
echo Arg-1 arg-2 arg-3 arg-4 arg-5 arg-6
Arg-1 arg-2 arg-3 arg-4 arg-5 arg-6
32% _
```

When used by itself, the **s** modifier affects only the first argument that it encounters on the command line. In the example, it changed **a** to **A** only in the first argument. To change **a** to **A** in **every** argument, use the global modifier **g** with **s**, as shown here:

```
32% !30:gs/a/A
echo Arg-1 Arg-2 Arg-3 Arg-4 Arg-5 Arg-6
Arg-1 Arg-2 Arg-3 Arg-4 Arg-5 Arg-6
33% _
```

To replace one argument only, include the argument number with the **s** modifier, as shown here:

```
33% !30:5:s/arg/ARG
echo ARG-5
ARG-5
34% _
```

In the example shown above, **30** identifies the event, **5** identifies the argument, and **s** performs the substitution.

Previewing an Event

You can preview an event without actually executing it by using the preview modifier **p**. The C shell will display the command line for you, as shown:

```
34% !30:p
echo arg.1 arg.2 arg.3 arg.4 arg.5 arg.6
35% _
```

You can also combine the preview modifier with other features. In the following example, we'll display only arguments 2, 3, and 4:

```
35% !30:2-4:p
echo arg.2 arg.3 arg.4
36% _
```

Abbreviating Your Commands _____

At the end of the **.cshrc** file described earlier in this chapter, you saw four **alias** commands on lines 3–6:

```
   % cat .cshrc
1. set prompt = "\!% "
2. set history = 12
3. alias ti        cd /usr/lib/terminfo/t
4. alias up        cd /usr/lib/uucppublic/pat
5. alias view      cd '\!*; ls -l ¦ more'
6. alias vt        vi /usr/pat/admin/totals
   % _
```

In this section, we'll describe these commands in greater detail. You will learn how to display a list of aliases, set up a temporary alias, and select arguments dynamically.

Listing Your Aliases

To display a list of your aliases, enter the **alias** command without an argument, as shown in this example:

```
36% alias
alias ti        cd /usr/lib/terminfo/t
alias up        cd /usr/lib/uucppublic/pat
alias view      cd '\!*; ls -l ¦ more'
alias vt        vi /usr/pat/admin/totals
37% _
```

The list displayed shows that you have four aliases: **ti**, **up**, **view**, and **vt**.

Using an Alias Temporarily

The aliases that you place in **.cshrc** are automatically activated every time you create a new C shell. To activate a special alias for one session, you can start it with the **alias** command, use it during the session, and then remove it with the **unalias** command. Here is a simple example:

```
40% alias cg cd /usr/greg/admin/goals
41% cg
 .
 .          {Work in /usr/greg/admin/goals}
 .
49% cd
50% cg
 .
 .          {Work in /usr/greg/admin/goals}
 .
63% cd
64% unalias cg
65% _
```

In command lines 40–65 above, you assign an alias called **cg** on line 40. You use the alias twice to move to the target directory, once on line 41 and then again on line 50. After each subsession in **/usr/greg/admin/goals**, you change back to your home directory (lines 49 and 63). Then, after finishing up your work in the other directory, you remove the alias on line 64.

Selecting Arguments Dynamically

On line 5 of **.cshrc**, we have an alias called **view**, which includes the notation for dynamic selection: \!*. Dynamic selection simply means that you can enter the name of the directory when you enter the command line. Here is the line as it appears in **.cshrc**:

```
alias view    cd '\!*; ls -l | more'
```

It's as if you left a space in the command line for the directory's name, as shown here:

```
alias view    cd directory; ls -l | more'
```

You fill in the name when you enter a command line, as shown in the following example:

```
65% view /usr/james/work/letters
cd /usr/james/work/letters; ls -l | more
total 25
-rwxr----- 1 james 6782 Feb  3 10:54 addendum
drwx--x--- 1 james  367 Mar 15 08:37 balance
-rw-r--r-- 2 james 9285 Apr 22 15:21 call-125
drwx------ 1 james  294 Jan 18 11:46 deadline
-rwxrw---- 1 james 8349 Dec 17 08:59 end.odd
-rw-rw-rw- 5 james 7956 May 24 10:03 first
66% _
```

Just below the command line, the C shell displays the command line with the name that you requested filled in. In place of \!*, you see the directory name **/usr/james/work/letters**. This feature allows you to use this alias with any name you choose.

## CHAPTER 12

MANAGING A SYSTEM

Introduction

In a single-user system like DOS, you have to perform administrative tasks like formatting your disks, backing up your files, setting up directories, and reducing fragmentation. But you don't have to learn a new set of commands or set aside a dedicated directory. You can make most adjustments, like the number of lines on the screen or the speed of your serial communication port, with relatively simple commands.

In a multiuser system like UNIX, system administration is an entire job of its own. It involves setting up accounts for users; taking care of terminals, printers, modems, disk drives, and tape drives; maintaining file systems; and setting file access permissions. In this chapter and the chapters that follow, we'll discuss these tasks in considerable detail.

The Job of a System Administrator

Anyone who does work on a DOS system is both user and system administrator combined. The same person runs application programs and backs up files. On a UNIX system, ordinary users run their application programs, while someone designated as system administrator takes care of those tasks that support the overall functioning of the system. The system administrator is often a full-time professional who takes care of the following:

- Formatting disks
- Setting up and closing accounts for users
- Keeping all hardware in working order
- Maintaining file systems and providing disk space for users
- Connecting the system to other UNIX systems
- Preventing unauthorized entry into the system
- Monitoring the use of the system to measure performance, implement billing, or maintain security

175

Descriptions of the tools for carrying out these tasks follow.

Logging In as System Administrator

A unique account is set aside for the system administrator. If you are logged in as an ordinary user, you can log into the system administrator's account by using the substitute user command **su**

```
$ su
Password:
#  _
```

If you are logged out, you can log directly into the system administrator's account, also known as the **root** account:

```
login: root
Password:
#  _
```

No matter how you log into this account, the shell begins displaying a different prompt (#). This prompt informs you that you are no longer logged in as an ordinary user; you are now the *super-user*, a name that describes the enlarged privileges granted to the system administrator.

The super-user is granted access to every directory and file in the system. If you are logged in as super-user, you can work within your system without restrictions. On a given system, only one person should be granted super-user status. Furthermore, if you are allowed to log in as super-user, you should do so only when you have administrative work to perform.

A Directory for the System Administrator

A separate directory called **/etc** contains most commands and files used by the system administrator, or super-user. In **/etc**, administrative commands are kept apart from the ordinary commands stored in **/bin** and **/usr/bin**. Even as super-user, you can still enter the full pathname for any command. However, to allow yourself to enter command names only, you can enter one of the following in your initialization file, which is **.login** for the Bourne shell or **.login** for the C shell:

```
Bourne shell

PATH=/etc:/bin:/usr/bin:$HOME/bin:
export PATH

        C shell

set path = (/etc /bin /usr/bin $HOME/bin .)
```

With one of these pathname statements in your initialization file, you will be able to enter commands without giving full pathnames.

System Initialization File

Just as each user, including the super-user, has an initialization file, so each UNIX system as a whole has its own initialization file, which is called **/etc/rc**. The letters **rc**, which occur often within a UNIX system, stand for "run commands." Just as the statements that you place in your own **.profile** or **.login** file are executed whenever you log in, the statements in **/etc/rc** are executed whenever the entire system is booted. We won't say any more about this file here, but we'll refer to it throughout the remainder of the book.

Getting Messages to Users

The users connected to your system may be in different locations, and you will have to communicate with them from time to time. Since the **mail** command is too slow, you will probably want to try one of the following:

- the write-all command, **wall**
- the **news** command
- the message of the day file, **/etc/motd**

The write-all command, **wall**, is similar to the **write** command. Your message will reach users very quickly but only those who are logged in at the moment. Here is an example:

```
# wall
The system will be down for maintenance at 3:00
CTRL D
#  _
```

A second possibility is to store a message in file **/usr/news** and then use the **news** command to send it to users.

A third choice is the message-of-the-day file, **/etc/motd**. Any message stored in this file is automatically displayed each time a user logs in. Here is an example:

```
# cat /etc/motd
All users will have to log out by 6:00 pm on Wednesday
#  _
```

To reply to a message from the system administrator, a user can use the electronic mail system to send a message to **root**, as illustrated in the following example:

```
$ mail root < disk_space
$ _
```

In this example, the message in file **disk_space** is mailed to the system administrator.

User Accounts

On a single-user system like DOS, you are the only user. On a multiuser system like UNIX, the system administrator is responsible for providing an account for each active user. The system administrator also keeps track of user activity. Keeping track of system users doesn't really have a counterpart in DOS.

The Password File

Information about authorized system users is stored in a file called **/etc/passwd**. For each user, you will find a one-line entry, which contains the following seven fields:

- User's login name
- User's encrypted password
- User identifier number
- Group identifier number
- Optional comments, such as the user's full name
- User's home directory
- User's login program, typically a command processor

The user's login name and password are the first two items the user enters when logging into the system. Although the user enters the password in the usual way, it always appears in the password encrypted. The user enters these in response to the opening prompts:

```
login:
Password:
```

The system uses the user and group identifiers, entered in the third and fourth fields, to identify processes and files. A group identifier, which is optional, indicates any working group to which the user may belong. The comments field, stored in the fifth field, allows you to read the **/etc/passwd** file more easily. The home directory, stored in the sixth field, is the directory into which the user initially logs in. The name of this directory is usually the subdirectory of **/usr** that has the user's login name.

The login program, stored in the sixth field, is the program that is active as soon as the user logs in. The program is usually one of the command processors, the Bourne shell or the C shell. However, for special accounts, it can be another program or no program.

The password file includes entries for the super-user, certain key processes, and also ordinary users. Each entry contains seven fields, separated from each other by colons (:), as shown in the following example:

```
root:i&8(wQm#EoVz:0:1:super-user:/:
daemon:x:1:1::/:
cron:x:1:3::/:
sys:PxtZ%3h'OmrWa:2:2:/sys:
bin:kMv7)e4AzPj1:3:2:/bin:
alex:Jy3*nZ3@mzU&sm:11:76:Alex Roberts:/usr/alex:/bin/csh
bill:Ud!9bw(SxMp,Ez:12:73:William Bowers:/usr/bill:/bin/sh
...
```

In the preceding example of a password file, the first entry for an ordinary user is on the sixth line. Only the last two lines shown above are for ordinary users. The entry for **alex** on the sixth line can be broken down into its seven fields as follows:

Number	Field Entry	Description
1	alex	User's login name
2	Jy3*nZ3@mzU&sm	User's encrypted password
3	11	User identifier
4	76	Group identifier
5	Alex Roberts	Comment: user's full name
6	/usr/alex	User's home directory
7	/bin/csh	Login program: the C shell

The Group File

If working groups are used on your system, they are described in a file called **/etc/group**. This file is similar to the password file, but it's a little simpler. Each line entry contains only four fields:

- Group name
- Encrypted password
- Group identifier
- A list of group members

Each group has its own name and password. The identifier entered here must match the identifier in the fourth field of each member's password entry. The list of members gives the login names of the members, separated by commas. Here is an example of a group file:

```
root:i&8(wQm#EoVz:1:root,daemon
```

```
sys:PxtZ%3h'OmrWa:2:sys,bin
mktg:Lm2)uWe5oKtZ:71:dan,edy,gary,kim
eng:Aqc4(eWzfGhrN:72:bill,cal,jan,pat
...
```

In the example shown above, the groups of ordinary users begin on the third line. Here is a breakdown of the third line into its four fields:

Number	Field Entry	Description
1	mktg	Group name
2	Lm2)uWe5oKtZ	Encrypted password
3	71	Group identifier
4	dan,edy,gary,kim	Members of the group

Setting Up a User Account

There are three, or possibly four, steps for the super-user to follow for adding a new user account to the system:

- Enter a line entry to **/etc/passwd**
- Enter a line entry to **/etc/group**, if required
- Give the user a home directory
- Place an initialization file in the user's home directory

Only the super-user can set up a new user account. Here are the steps in more detail:

1. Enter a line to the system password file:
   a. Start an editing session at the end of **/etc/passwd**:

```
# pwd
/etc
# vi + passwd
```

   b. Enter a line for the new user account:

```
a
bill:Ud!9bw(SxMp,Ez:12:73:William Bowers:/usr/bill:/bin/sh
ESC
```

The line entry shown above makes the Bourne shell the login program. To make the C shell the login program, use **/bin/csh** instead of **/bin/sh**.

   c. Leave **vi** and return to the shell prompt:

```
:wq
#
```

2. Give the new user a home directory:
   a. Create the new directory in **/usr**:

   ```
   # cd /usr
   # mkdir bill
   # _
   ```

   b. Change ownership of the directory from **root** to **bill**:

   ```
   # chown bill bill
   # _
   ```

   c. Change the group identifier to **73**:

   ```
   # chgrp 73 /usr/bill
   # _
   ```

3. Construct an initialization file in the new directory:
   a. Log into the new account:

   ```
   # login bill
   Password:
   $ _
   ```

   b. Begin an editing session with **vi**:

   ```
   $ vi + .profile
   ```

   If the new user has the C shell, use **.login** instead of **.profile**.
   c. Provide pathnames for commands and electronic mail:

   ```
   a
   PATH=:/bin:/usr/bin:/usr/bill/bin:
   MAIL=/usr/mail/bill
   ```

   d. Identify and set the new user's terminal:

   ```
   TERM=vt100
   stty erase '^h' kill '^z'
   ```

e. Export the three shell variables (Bourne shell only):

```
export PATH, MAIL, TERM
ESC
```

f. Leave **vi** and return to the shell prompt:

```
:wq
$ _
```

At this point, you can use **su** to leave this account and return to super-user status.

Determining Who Is Logged In

The **who** command tells you which users are logged in at any given moment. It displays the login name, terminal, and the date and time when the user logged in. Anyone can use this command, but it can be especially useful to the system administrator. Here is an example:

```
$ who
allen        tty14        Feb 16 07:56
ben          tty03        Feb 16 09:14
carl         tty11        Feb 16 08:37
dana         tty08        Feb 15 10:23
edy          tty15        Feb 16 09:44
fred         tty09        Feb 16 09:08
gwen         tty12        Feb 15 10:18
$ _
```

The information displayed by the **who** command comes from a file called /**etc/utmp**. Each line of the display, as shown above, identifies one user who is currently logged in.

If you want more information, you can use various options with the **who** command. For example, the **-u** option also provides the amount of time since the user's last activity and the process identifier (PID) of the user's shell. Here is an example:

```
$ who
allen   tty14   Feb 16 07:56   2:32    29175
ben     tty03   Feb 16 09:14   5:16    37829
carl    tty11   Feb 16 08:37   1:28    33048
dana    tty08   Feb 15 10:23    .      12931
edy     tty15   Feb 16 09:44   3:54    38294
fred    tty09   Feb 16 09:08    .      36942
gwen    tty12   Feb 15 10:18    .      12855
$ _
```

A dot (.) in the time column means the user has done something within the last minute; "old" means the terminal has been inactive for at least 24 hours.

Processes That Run Themselves _____

In this section you will learn about processes that start themselves and processes that you can schedule to be run using the system's built-in timer.

Daemon Processes

A number of key functions in the operation of a UNIX system are carried out by processes that appear to run automatically on their own. These processes, referred to as *daemons*, take care of many queues by running themselves in the background. (The term daemon came into UNIX vernacular by way of the PDP-7 minicomputer, on which UNIX was run during the early years of its development.)

For example, daemons are used to send printing jobs in the **lp** queue to the appropriate printer, forward messages that have been sent by electronic mail, and perform all the different tasks required by the **uucp** network. Just start these processes when you start the system, and they run themselves on their own schedules.

To start any daemon, you can either enter it manually from the command line or place it in an initialization file. For example, a daemon called **update** automatically keeps all your disks up to date every 30 seconds. One possibility is to enter this command on a command line:

```
#  /etc/update &
#  _
```

The other possibility is to place this command in your **/etc/rc** file, which is executed each time the system is booted. This second method is preferable to the first. There are just too many commands that need to be started with the system, and you may not be able to remember them all.

The UNIX System Timer

A command called **cron** gives you a system timer, allowing you to have commands run at various times of the day, week, or month. It's something like an alarm clock or a timer on a video cassette recorder (VCR). Just place the appropriate lines of information in a file called **/usr/lib/crontab**, and the **cron** command takes care of the rest. (You will probably want to start **cron** in your **/etc/rc** file.)

Each line entry in **/usr/lib/crontab** gives a starting time (or a series of times) and a command to be executed. Once you have the file set up, **cron** starts each command at the time (or times) you requested. You enter times using numbers in five fields (minute, hour, day of month, month, and day of week). The system timer runs according to a 24-hour clock, using these permissible numeric values:

Minute	Hour	Day of Month	Month	Day of Week
0-59	0-23	1-31	1-12	0-6

The 24-hour clock begins at midnight. That is, 0000 represents midnight, while 1200 represents noon. Then 0100 means 1:00 AM, while 1300 means 1:00 PM. Days of the week begin with Sunday (zero) and end on Saturday (six). That is, 0 means Sunday, 1 means Monday, 2 means Tuesday, and so on. You can enter an asterisk (*) in any of these fields to mean "all times." For example, an asterisk in the hour field means "every hour."

Use blank spaces or tabs to separate each field from the previous field. Use a pound sign (#) to begin a comment. Here is a simple example of a line entry for the **/usr/lib/crontab** file. This entry causes the contents of a file called **/etc/today** to be displayed on the console (terminal zero) every weekday morning at 9:30:

```
30   9   *   *   1-5     cat /etc/today > /dev/tty00
```

In the preceding example, the first two numbers give the time in reverse order ("30 9" means 9:30 AM); the pair of asterisks that follow mean "every day of every month; and "1-5" means Monday through Friday.

In the next example, we'll cause a brief reminder to be mailed to the system administrator on the fifth of every month:

```
15   8   5   *   *     echo "Statements due" | mail root
```

In the preceding example, "15 8" means 8:15 AM; "5 *" means the fifth of every month; and the final asterisk means to perform the task any day of the week, wherever the fifth falls.

Many statements used in the **crontab** file involve the **find** command, which allows you to locate and weed out various files and directories. Here is an example:

```
0   2   *   *   1,3,5   find / -name core -atime +3 -exec rm {} \;
```

In the previous statement, "0 2" means 2:00 AM, and "1,3,5" means Monday, Wednesday, and Friday. Every Monday, Wednesday, and Friday morning at 2:00 AM, the system will locate and remove all files named **core** that haven't been accessed for at least three days.

The next example is very similar to the one just shown:

```
30  2  *  *  *       find /tmp /usr/tmp -atime +5 -exec rm {} \;
```

In the preceding example, the system locates and removes all temporary files (those found in directories **/tmp** and **/usr/tmp**) that haven't been accessed for at least five days.

The final example is also similar to the two previous examples:

```
0  3  *  *  *       find / -type d -size +6 -print | lp
```

In the preceding example, every morning at 3:00 AM the system searches for directories larger than 6 kbytes and prints a list of them for the system administrator.

You can use comments to provide a set of headings or a blank line:

```
# cat /usr/lib/crontab
# mm hh dd mo  dw            Command
#
 30  9  *  *  1-5  cat /etc/today > /dev/tty00
  0  2  *  *  1,3,5 find / -name core -atime +3 -exec rm {} \;
 30  2  *  *  *    find /tmp /usr/tmp -atime +5 -exec rm {} \;
  0  3  *  *  *    find / -type d -size +6 -print | lp
 15  8  5  *  *    echo "Statements due" | mail root
$ _
```

Permissions For The System Administrator _____

Using Mnemonic Symbols

In Chapter 3, "Files and Directories," you changed file access permissions with the change mode command, **chmod**. For example, suppose you have a file called **permit**. To allow other users to read **permit**, you can execute the following:

```
$ chmod o+r permit
$ _
```

Then you can display the changed permission for the file by using the **ls −l** command, as illustrated below:

```
$ ls -l permit
-rwxrw-r-- 1 bill    283 Jan 18 10:43 permit
$ _
```

Using Numbers

The line displayed in the previous example by the **ls-l**command shows file access permissions in mnemonic symbols. That is, **r** means read, **w** means write, **x** means execute, and so on. This notation is reasonably clear to ordinary users. But a system administrator must also work with numeric notation. Table 12-1 shows the translation of the permissions shown above from mnemonic to numeric notation.

Table 12-1. Equivalent Permission Symbols

Description	Owner	Group	Others
Mnemonic notation	r w x	r w -	r - -
Binary equivalent	1 1 1	1 1 0	1 0 0
Octal translation	7	6	4

As Table 12-1 shows, each permission granted represents a binary 1 and each permission denied, a binary 0. The octal translation of the binary string is equivalent to the mnemonic string. In Table 12-1, **rwxrw-r--** is equivalent to **764**.

When you enter a **chmod** command line, you can use either a mnemonic or a numeric argument, depending on your preference. Experienced users generally prefer numeric arguments. Assuming the access permissions described previously, the following two command lines are identical:

```
$ chmod o+r permit          $ chmod 764 permit
$ _                         $ _
```

Converting to Octal

Numeric arguments for the **chmod** command are given in base 8, or *octal*, numbers. It is very easy to convert numbers from base 2, or *binary*, numbers to octal because of the mathematical relationship between the two number bases. Since 8 is the third power of 2, each three binary digits are equivalent to one octal digit, as shown in Table 12-2.

Table 12-2. Binary to Octal Conversion

Binary	Octal	Binary	Octal
0 0 0	0	1 0 0	4
0 0 1	1	1 0 1	5
0 1 0	2	1 1 0	6
0 1 1	3	1 1 1	7

Referring to Table 12-2, the left digit is worth 4, the middle digit is worth 2, and the right digit is worth 1. Using the example in Table 12-1, you can translate the owner access permissions as shown here:

```
1. Mnemonic string                    r      w      x
2. Binary representation              1      1      1
3. Value of each digit                4      2      1
                                   ------------------
4. Value of string (line 2 x line 3)  4      2      1
5. Octal translation (sum of
   values on line 4)                         7
```

Here is the same computation for the group permissions:

```
1. Mnemonic string                    r      w      -
2. Binary representation              1      1      0
3. Value of each digit                4      2      1
                                   ------------------
4. Value of string (line 2 x line 3)  4      2      0
5. Octal translation (sum of
   values on line 4)                         6
```

Here is the same computation for the other permissions:

```
1. Mnemonic string                    r      -      -
2. Binary representation              1      0      0
3. Value of each digit                4      2      1
                                   ------------------
4. Value of string (line 2 x line 3)  4      0      0
5. Octal translation (sum of
   values on line 4)                         4
```

Here are some more examples of file access permissions translated from mnemonic to numeric notation:

```
r-- --- ---      rw- rw- ---      rwx r-x ---
100 000 000      110 110 000      111 101 000
 4   0   0        6   6   0        7   5   0

rw- r-- r--      rwx rw- -w-      rwx rwx rwx
110 100 100      111 110 010      111 111 111
 6   4   4        7   6   2        7   7   7
```

As the preceding examples demonstrate, the lowest possible octal permission is 000 (all access denied), the lowest realistic permission is 400, and the highest is 777 (total access).

CHAPTER 13

MANAGING DISKS AND TAPES

In DOS, adding a new disk or tape drive is fairly simple. You simply install the device in its space and the controller board in its slot. Then, in certain instances, you enter a line in your system's **CONFIG.SYS** file. For example, suppose you add a 3.5-inch disk drive to your system as drive B. You mount the drive, connect it to your power supply, and insert the controller board (unless it runs off an existing controller board). Then, to inform DOS that you now have a 3.5-inch disk drive, you add the following line to your **CONFIG.SYS** file:

```
DEVICE = \SYS\DOS\DRIVER.SYS /B:1
```

From now on, you can refer to this drive in DOS commands as **B:**. You can copy files to and from this drive by using its new name. Here is an example for copying files from your 3.5-inch disk drive to your hard drive (**C:**):

```
C:\> COPY B:*.*
```

In UNIX, the job is a little more involved. Disk and tape drives do not have simple one-letter names as they do in DOS. Each drive is integrated into the UNIX system by a process known as *mounting*. When a drive is mounted on a UNIX system, it assumes a place in the file system. Mounting means locating the drive in a specific place in the directory tree. Once it's been mounted, you refer to it only by the directory (or directories) represented by the drive. In UNIX, each user refers only to files and directories, not to particular drives.

All in all, adding a new drive to a UNIX system is more demanding for the system administrator but easier for ordinary users. Users don't need to be aware of the locations of the system's hardware devices. They can refer to files and directories without having to know exactly where they are located on the hardware.

Devices And File Types

So far, you have worked only with two types of files: ordinary files and directories. But in UNIX, devices are also represented as files, and there are three other types of files, which are called *special files*. So we'll begin with devices.

Devices in the UNIX System

Like DOS, UNIX supports a number of peripheral devices, including terminals, printers, modems, disk drives, and magnetic tape drives. Unlike DOS, however, UNIX represents each device as a file in the device directory /**dev**.

Each device connected to a UNIX system is identified by two numbers: a **major device number** (which gives the general type of device) and a **minor device number** (which distinguishes this device from others of the same type). Major device numbers are not standardized, and vary widely from one UNIX installation to another. However, a typical numbering scheme could look like this:

0	Local terminal	5	Tape (block)
1	Remote terminal	6	Diskette (block)
2	Line printer	7	Raw disk (character)
3	Character printer	8	Raw tape (character)
4	Hard disk (block)	9	Diskette (character)

Using the numbering scheme shown above for major device numbers (which is not standard), terminal number 5 (tty05) would have a major device number of 0 (local terminal) and a minor device number of 5. Line printer number 3 would have a major device number of 2 (line printer) and a minor device number of 3.

Devices that require human interaction, such as terminals, modems, and printers, process one character at a time. These are known as *character devices* (or *asynchronous devices*). Mass storage devices, such as disk and tape drives, store data in larger units called blocks. These are known as *block devices*. As explained in the subsection that follows, a file that represents a device must match the device type.

Special Files

Every UNIX system has a device directory called /**dev** set aside for *special files*, the files that represent hardware devices. Before System V, Release 2, all special files were stored in the main directory. As of Release 2, /**dev** has four subdirectories dedicated to mass storage devices—two for disk drives and two for tape drives. In each case, one directory is for drives to be used as block devices and the other is for drives to be used as character (raw) devices. The names of the four subdirectories of /**dev** are as follows:

- **dsk**—for hard drives to be used as block devices
- **rdsk**—for hard drives to be used as character (raw) devices
- **mt**—for magnetic tape drives to be used as block devices
- **rmt**—for magnetic tape drives to be used as character (raw) devices

The **r** in the second and fourth names stands for **raw** device, which is the same as a character device. Each actual device is represented twice in directory /**dev**—once as a block device and once as a character device. This allows you to access disk and tape drives without blocking when necessary.

File Types

Hardware devices connected to a UNIX system are regarded as files (special files, to be exact). Two special file types relate to hardware devices: block and character. A third special file type, of interest only to system programmers, is the *fifo* (first in, first out) file—also called a *named pipe*. All together, there are five file types found in a UNIX system, with the following names and letter codes:

- − Ordinary files (text, programs, and data)
- d Directories (collections of files)
- b Block special files (mass storage devices)
- c Character special files (asynchronous devices)
- p Fifo special files (named pipes)

Block (b) and character (c) special files are found only in the device directory /**dev**.

More on Directory Listings

You learned the basic functions of the list command **ls** in Chapter 3, "Files and Directories." Now that you know more about file types, let's talk more about displaying directory listings. In addition to permissions, number of links, file size, and time of last modification, the **ls −l** displays a one-character file type, using one of the characters listed in the previous subsection. Two other options you can bundle with the −l option are:

−a	Display all names (even those that begin with periods)
−s	Display file sizes in blocks

Here are some directory listings that include these options:

1. Display all files in the current directory:
   a. Bundle long with all:

```
$ ls -al
total 150
drwxr-xr-x  66 bin     Section   1056 Sep 14 21:55 .
drwxr-xr-x  17 bin     bin        752 Sep 15 05:01 ..
-rwx------   1 don     Section    232 Apr 28 13:25 .login
drwxr-xr-x   6 adrian  Dept-A5    816 Sep 14 20:16 adrian
drwxr-xr-x   3 andysar Delta-D    144 May 27 17:41 andysar
drwxr-xr-x   2 artel   Section     48 Aug 23 10:35 artel
...
$ _
```

   b. This listing includes the directory's link to itself (.), its link to the parent directory (..), and the C shell's initialization file **.login**.

2. Display block sizes:
   a. Bundle long with size:

```
$ ls -als
total 150
   4 drwxr-xr-x  66 bin     Section   1056 Sep 14 21:55 .
   2 drwxr-xr-x  17 bin     bin        752 Sep 15 05:01 ..
   1 -rwx------   1 don     Section    232 Apr 28 13:25 .login
   2 drwxr-xr-x   6 adrian  Dept-A5    816 Sep 14 20:16 adrian
   2 drwxr-xr-x   3 andysar Delta-D    144 May 27 17:41 andysar
   2 drwxr-xr-x   2 artel   Section     48 Aug 23 10:35 artel
 ... $ _
```

3. Display the major directories in root:
   a. Give the long listing:

```
$ ls -l /
total 2576
drwxrwxr-x   2 bin     bin       2704 Sep 10 15:20 bin
-r--------   1 bin     bin      26006 Aug 23 07:17 boot
-rw-------   1 root    root       233 Sep 14 02:14 dead.letter
drwxr-xr-x   2 bin     bin       6144 Sep  3 19:37 dev
-r--------   1 bin     bin        577 Dec 29  1988 dos
drwxr-xr-x   5 bin     bin       2048 Sep 15 20:58 etc
drwxr-xr-x   5 bin     bin       1168 Aug 24 13:31 lib
drwx--x--x   2 bin     bin       7168 May 27 20:43 lost+found
drwxr-xr-x   2 bin     bin         32 May  9  1988 mnt
drwxrwxrwx   2 bin     bin       1056 Sep 15 20:58 tmp
drwxr-xr-x  28 bin     bin       2160 Sep 12 19:37 usr
-r-x------   1 sysinfo bin     279304 Aug 28 19:35 xenix
$ _
```

   b. All files are shown with block sizes.

4. Display the contents of the device directory:
   a. Use the long option alone in a XENIX system:

```
$ ls -l /dev
total 1456
brw-rw-rw-   4 bin     bin      2, 36 Dec 29  1988 fd048
brw-rw-rw-   1 root    root     2, 12 Dec 29  1988 fd048ds8
brw-rw-rw-   4 bin     bin      2, 36 Dec 29  1988 fd048ds9
brw-------   1 sysinfo sysinfo  1,  0 Dec 29  1988 hd00
brw-------   1 sysinfo sysinfo  1, 15 Dec 29  1988 hd01
crw-------   1 sysinfo sysinfo  4,  1 Dec 29  1988 kmem
```

```
c-w--w--w-    2 bin       bin       6,   1 Sep 14 22:31 lp
c-w--w--w-    1 bin       bin       6,   0 May  3 20:56 lp0
c-w--w--w-    2 bin       bin       6,   1 Sep 14 22:31 lp1
crw-------    1 sysinfo   sysinfo   4,   0 Dec 29   1988 mem
crw-rw-rw-    4 bin       bin       2,  36 Jun 11 22:00 rfd048
crw-rw-rw-    1 root      root      2,  12 Dec 29   1988 rfd048ds8
crw-rw-rw-    4 bin       bin       2,  36 Jun 11 22:00 rfd048ds9
crw-------    1 sysinfo   sysinfo   1,   0 Dec 29   1988 rhd00
crw-------    1 sysinfo   sysinfo   1,  15 Dec 29   1988 rhd01
crw-rw-rw-    1 bin       bin       3,   0 Sep 15 15:57 tty
crw-rw----    1 uucp      root     10,   0 Sep  7 06:24 tty000
crw-rw----    1 uucp      root     10,   1 Sep  7 06:22 tty001
crw-rw----    1 uucp      root     10,   2 Sep  7 06:21 tty002
crw-rw----    1 uucp      root     10,   3 Sep  7 06:19 tty003
$ _
```

b. Device numbers replace the sizes in bytes.

Other options for the **ls** command that may be of interest to system administrators are as follows:

−n	Same as **−l**, but display owner and group identifiers instead of the filename
−t	Sort by time of last modification
−tu	Sort by time of last access

Adding And Removing Devices

To add a hardware device to a UNIX system, begin by identifying the device. If the device is a disk drive, then you have to add a file system. Adding a disk drive requires the use of four different commands.

Creating a Device File

Begin by creating a device file in **/dev** using the make node command, **mknod**. The **mknod** command requires four arguments:

- Filename
- File type
- Major device number
- Minor device number

Using the major device numbers shown earlier in this chapter (which are not standard for UNIX systems), you could set up terminal number 5 with this command:

```
#/etc/mknod /dev/tty05 c 0 5
#_
```

In the preceding example, the filename for this terminal is **/dev/tty05**, the file type is special character (c), the major device number is 0, and the minor device number is 5. All four arguments except the third are standard for all UNIX systems. The major device number will be different for each system. If you have your pathnames for commands set up in your initialization file, it won't be necessary to use the full pathname of the command (**/etc/mknod**). You can just enter **mknod**.

In the next example, we'll create two device files for magnetic tape drive 1—one to define a block device and one to define a character device. According to the list shown near the beginning of this chapter, the major device numbers for this hypothetical system are 5 and 8:

```
# /etc/mknod /dev/mt/1 b 5 1
# /etc/mknod /dev/rmt/1 c 8 1
# _
```

In the preceding examples, the device filenames are **/dev/mt/1** and **/dev/rmt/1**, the file types are block (**b**) and character (**c**), the major device numbers are **5** and **8**, and the minor device numbers are both **1**. Again, the major device numbers will vary greatly from one UNIX system to another.

For our third example, we'll set up a pair of device files for hard disk drive 3. This example will be very similar to the previous example, except that the filenames will be more complicated. With disk drives, the name must be of the form

$$cCdDsS$$

where   **cC** is the controller number (C)
            dD is the disk number (D)
            sS is the slice (partition) number (P)

Here are the examples:

```
# /etc/mknod /dev/dsk/c0d1s3 b 4 3
# /etc/mknod /dev/rdsk/c0d1s3 c 7 3
# _
```

In XENIX, the notation is a little different. Diskettes (floppy disks) begin with the letters fd (or rfd); hard disks begin with the letters hd (or rhd). For diskettes, the name includes the number of tracks, the number of sides, and the number of sectors, as shown here:

$$fdtracksdssectors$$

or

$$fdtrackssssectors$$

where   *tracks* is the number of tracks
ds means double sided
ss means single sided
sectors is the number of sectors

Here are examples for a diskette drive on a XENIX system:

```
#  /etc/mknod /dev/fd048ds9 b 6 3
#  /etc/mknod /dev/rfd048ds9 c 9 3
#  _
```

If you are installing a terminal, modem, or printer, the next step is to go on to the appropriate chapter ("Managing Terminals," 14, or "Managing Printers," 15). If you are installing a disk drive, continue following the procedures described in the rest of this chapter. Most tape drives won't require any further steps, either.

Formatting the Disk

The next step for a disk drive is to format the disk. A special utility program, provided with the disk, will mark the sectors for reading and writing of data. The name of the program and the procedure for running it will vary from one manufacturer to another. This is a departure from DOS, which has a single **FORMAT** program included in the operating system.

As most DOS users know, a new disk is completely blank, and cannot be used in a computer system. Formatting is required to identify usable locations on the surface. Then programs can store data in these locations and read data already stored.

A diskette that has been formatted contains a series of concentric rings of read/write space known as **tracks**. Each track is organized into smaller areas called **sectors**. Track and sector numbers are used to locate data on a formatted disk.

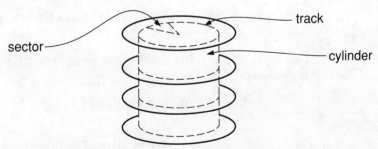

Figure 13-1. Tracks, Sectors, and Cylinders

Larger drives with multiple disks also have **cylinders**. A cylinder is a set of tracks on different disks, all the same distance from the edge. Together, these tracks form a cylindrical shape in space. If a drive has four disks with 80 tracks on each surface, there will be 80 cylinders.

Since each disk has two sides, this drive will have eight surfaces. Since one surface is usually used for servo control information, that leaves seven read/write surfaces and seven read/write heads.

Creating a File System

After you've formatted your disk, you have to create a file system with the **mkfs** command. The command requires two arguments: the name of the special file and the number of blocks needed. The filename is the same one you used with the **mknod** command. In the following example, you create a file system for magnetic tape drive 1 with 20,000 blocks:

```
# /etc/mkfs /dev/rmt/1 20000
# _
```

In the next example, you create a file system for hard disk drive 3 with 56,000 blocks:

```
# /etc/mkfs /dev/dsk/c0d1s3 56000
# _
```

Creating a Label

In DOS, the /V option of the **FORMAT** command allows you to give a formatted disk an 11-character volume name. In UNIX, you can do something similar with the **labelit** command. If you use this optional command, you can assign a six-character file system identifier and a six-character volume identifier. In the following example, you identify the file system for magnetic tape 1 as tape01 and the volume as sales:

```
# /etc/labelit /dev/mt/1 tape01 sales
# _
```

In the next example, you identify the file system of disk drive 3 as **disk03** and the volume as **tests**:

```
# /etc/labelit /dev/dsk/c0d1s3 disk03 tests
# _
```

You can display existing identifiers by using the **labelit** command followed only by the name of the file system.

Mounting a File System

The last step in adding a disk or tape drive is to mount it on the system with the **mount** command. This command allows you to select the location of the device's file system, which will be added to a list in a file called **/etc/mounttab** (mount table). For write-protected devices, to avoid errors, you must include the read-only option (−**r**) at the end of the command line. In the following example, you mount write-protected magnetic tape drive 1 as **/usr/tape01**:

```
# pwd
/usr
# mkdir tape01
# /etc/mount /dev/mt/1 /usr/tape01 -r
# _
```

The command shown above assigns to the device file (**/dev/mt/1**) the directory called **/usr/tape01**. The **-r** option is required for a write-protected device. In the next example, you mount hard disk drive 3 at **/usr/results**:

```
# pwd
/usr
# mkdir results
# /etc/mount /dev/dsk/c0d1s3 /usr/results
# _
```

You can display file systems currently mounted by entering the **mount** command by itself. Beginning with System V, Release 3, you can mount a file system on another UNIX system with the −**d** option using the Remote File Sharing (RFS) feature.

Unmounting a File System

To remove a device from a UNIX system, use the unmount command, **umount**. (In keeping with UNIX tradition, the first **n** has been omitted from the command. The name of the command is **umount**, not **unmount**.) To unmount magnetic tape drive 1, use the device name:

```
# /etc/umount /dev/mt/1
# _
```

To unmount disk drive 3, use a command like this:

```
# /etc/umount /dev/dsk/c0d1s3
# _
```

The order to follow for mounting and unmounting devices is:

1. Connect the device
2. Mount the device on the file system
3. Use the device on the system
4. Unmount the device
5. Disconnect the device

If you don't follow this order, you can damage a device.

Backing Up To Tape or Disk

In DOS, you can use XCOPY or a commercial application program like Fastback to back up your files. In UNIX, there are several programs included in the system. The one that gives you the most control and versatility is the copy input/output program, **cpio**.

Copy Input/Output

The **cpio** program has three functions, each selected by an argument on the command line called a **key**. The three keys and the functions they select are as follows:

Key	Function
−p	Pass. Copy files from one directory to another.
−o	Output. Copy files from a directory to a storage device (usually a disk or tape drive).
−i	Input. Copy files from a storage device to a directory.

The **−p** option is for selective copying within the system, **−o** is for backup, and **−i** is for recovery.

Command Options

The **cpio** command has quite a few options that you can use with each key. The most common options are shown in Table 13-1.

You can use some options with all keys, but many options are restricted to use with one or two keys. To use any key, bundle it with the key on the command line. For example, to list filenames while copying them from one directory to another, type **cpio−pv** on the command line. The format of a **cpio** command line differs somewhat for each key. So we'll have to look at each key and its function separately.

Table 13-1. Options for cpio

Option	Purpose
B	Block. Write to tape in blocks of 5,120 bytes per block (output and input keys only).
d	Directory. Create any directories that may be required for copying (input and pass keys only).
l	Link. Link the files instead of copying them (passkey only).
t	Table of contents. Display filenames without copying (all keys).
v	Verbose. Display the name of each file that is copied (all keys).

Passing Files

If you want to copy files from one directory to another, use the **−p** key. Suppose your home directory, **/usr/don**, includes a work directory called **work**, along with two subdirectories, and a backup directory called **backup**, as shown in Figure 13-2.

Suppose you want to copy files to your **backup** directory. If you want to copy only the files in **work** itself, excluding its two subdirectories, you can use the **ls** command to pipe filenames into the **cpio** command, as shown here:

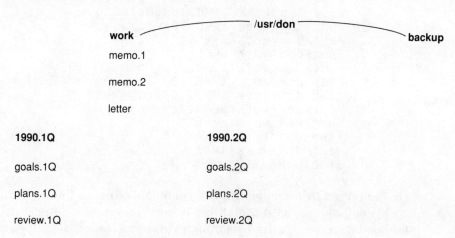

Figure 13-2. Sample Home Directory

```
$ pwd
/usr/don/work
$ ls | cpio -p ../backup
10 blocks
$ _
```

In the preceding example, the **cpio** receives a list of filenames from the **ls** command and passes (copies) these files to the target directory (/**usr**/**don**/ **backup**). The **cpio** command copies the files and displays the number of blocks copied.

It's often more helpful to see the names of the files being copied. To do this, just add the verbose option **v** to the key, as shown here:

```
$ pwd
/usr/don/work
$ ls | cpio -pv ../backup
/usr/don/work/memo1
/usr/don/work/memo.2
/usr/don/work/letter
10 blocks
$ _
```

On the other hand, you may want to copy all files in the current directory, along with all files in subdirectories of the current directory. In this example, that would mean the three files in **work**, together with the three files in **1990.1Q** and the three in **1990.2Q**. Use **find** instead of **ls**, as shown below:

```
$ pwd
/usr/don/work
$ find . -print | cpio -pv ../backup
/usr/don/work/1990.1Q/goals.1Q
/usr/don/work/1990.1Q/plans.1Q
/usr/don/work/1990.1Q/review.1Q
/usr/don/work/1990.1Q
/usr/don/work/1990.2Q/goals.2Q
/usr/don/work/1990.2Q/plans.2Q
/usr/don/work/1990.2Q/review.2Q
/usr/don/work/1990.2Q
/usr/don/work/memo1
/usr/don/work/memo.2
/usr/don/work/letter
32 blocks $ _
```

In the preceding example, the **find** command searches the current directory (.) and produces a list of all files, including those in subdirectories. The **cpio** command receives this list through a pipe and copies each file named in the list to the target directory (/**usr**/**don**/**backup**).

Copying Files Out to Devices

Backing up files on a storage device is similar to passing them to another directory. The main difference, of course, is that you use the output key, **−o**, instead of the pass key, **−p**. Two other differences are that the **−p** key requires redirection of output and that the target directory is a special file rather than a directory file. Here is an example for backing up files in the current directory to a hard disk:

```
$ pwd
/usr/don/work
$ ls ¦ cpio -o > /dev/rdsk/c0d1s3
10 blocks
$ _
```

The example shown above is similar to the first example for passing files from directory to directory.

When you use the output key **−o**, you can also request filenames by including the verbose option **v**:

```
$ pwd
/usr/don/work
$ ls ¦ cpio -ov > /dev/rdsk/c0d1s3
/usr/don/work/memo1
/usr/don/work/memo.2
/usr/don/work/letter
10 blocks
$ _
```

In most of your work, you will probably use the verbose option, **−v**. However, to save space, we'll omit it from the rest of the examples in this section.

If you are backing up to a tape drive, you will probably want to request the option for blocking, **−B**, as shown here:

```
$ pwd
/usr/don/work
$ ls ¦ cpio -oB > /dev/rmt/3
10 blocks
$ _
```

Finally, to copy all files in this directory, including those in subdirectories, use **find** instead of **ls** to provide the list of files:

```
$ pwd
/usr/don/work
$ find . -print ¦ cpio -oB > /dev/rmt/3
32 blocks
$ _
```

If it should become necessary to restore your entire directory, a backup like the one just shown is best, because it includes the entire directory intact.

Copying Files Into Directories

You can recover files only after you've previously backed them up. That is, you can use the input key −i only after you've used the output key −o. In this subsection, we'll consider recovering files that you've already backed up in the previous subsection. We'll begin with files backed up to a hard disk:

```
$ pwd
/usr/don/work
$ ls ¦ cpio -i < /dev/rdsk/c0d1s3
32 blocks
$ _
```

The example shown above is nearly identical to the corresponding example shown earlier for backing up these files. There are only two differences: now we are using the input key, −i, and we are redirecting input instead of output.

To recover files from a tape drive, include a request for blocking:

```
$ pwd
/usr/don/work
$ ls ¦ cpio -iB < /dev/rmt/3
32 blocks
$ _
```

Other Programs

This concludes our discussion of the **cpio** program. We'll end this chapter with a few words about other UNIX programs available for backup and recover.

In this chapter, you learned about the **cpio** program. But there are also four other programs you can use for backup, recovery, and archive, as shown in Table 13-2.

Table 13-2. Copy and Archive Programs

Program	Description
dd	A copy program that can also convert files from format to format or standard to standard.
tar	Tape archive: a program for both backup and recovery using tape or diskette. It is easier to use than **cpio** but less versatile.
cpio	The copy program for both backup and recovery, which can be used in conjunction with **find** to select files with great accuracy.
dump	A backup program, used with **restor**, that permits nine levels of backup from 0 (the entire system) to 9 (only the most recently modified files).
restor	A restoration program that restores files backed up with **dump**.
volcopy	Volume copy: copies entire file systems, not selected files, to disk or tape.

Some of these programs have serious limitations. For example, the **dump** program can't detect end of tape, and the **restor** program isn't very good at selecting individual files. Overall, the most useful program of the group is probably **cpio**, with its considerable versatility and precision.

## CHAPTER 14

MANAGING TERMINALS

Introduction

Adjustments Under DOS

When you use DOS, you usually have only one "terminal," and that terminal is usually built into your computer system. You probably don't even think of it as a terminal. However, you can make a few minor adjustments to its screen display.

Your terminal's display probably conforms to one of six IBM standards developed during the 1980s as shown in Table 14-1.

Table 14-1. Display Standards

Common Name	Full Name and Comments
MDA	Monochrome Display Adapter. Monochrome, medium resolution, text only.
Hercules	Monochrome, medium resolution, text and graphics.
CGA	Color/Graphics Adapter. Color, low resolution, text and graphics.
EGA	Enhanced Graphics Adapter. Color, medium resolution, text and graphics.
MCGA	Multi-Color Graphics Array. Color, medium resolution, text and graphics.
VGA	Video Graphics Array. Color, high resolution, text and graphics.

The MODE command allows you to control the screen display in several ways. If you have a CGA display, you can switch the display back and forth between 40 and 80 columns. To switch from 40 to 80, you could use the following command:

```
C:\> MODE CON 80
C:\> _
```

If you have both monochrome and CGA, you can switch back and forth between them, with four choices for the CGA display: 40 columns (color on or off) and 80 columns (color on or off). Here are the arguments you can use with the MODE command:

```
MONO        Monochrome
BW40        40-column CGA, color off
CO40        40-column CGA, color on
BW80        80-column CGA, color off
CO80        80-column CGA, color on
```

To switch to a CGA display with 80 columns and color turned off, you could use the following command:

```
C:\> MODE CON BW80
```

Beginning with version 4 of DOS, if you have an EGA or VGA display, you can specify the number of columns and lines in the display. If you want to display only 40 characters per line, you can use the following command:

```
C:\> MODE CON COLS=40
c:\> _
```

To display 80 columns and 48 lines, you can use a command like this:

```
C:\> MODE CON COLS-80 LINES=48
C:\> _
```

Adjustments Under UNIX

The DOS MODE command is a general-purpose command that controls many different hardware devices. UNIX has a command called **stty** (set terminal), which is roughly analogous to the DOS MODE command. The **stty** command, however, is used only for terminals, not for any other devices. To make adjustments to other devices, you have to use different commands.

For programs like **vi** that require a full-screen display, there is also a database for terminal information. There is a file in every UNIX system that contains descriptions of terminal functions for a large number of terminals. Before you can use **vi**, you have to find the name of your terminal in the file and assign it to the shell's terminal variable.

Basic Terminal Settings

Because a terminal in a UNIX system is viewed as a remote peripheral device, rather than an integrated part of the host computer, there are far more choices for you to make. To begin with, the file **/etc/gettydefs** contains default settings for terminals. If you don't request any settings at all, the settings in this file will be in effect. However, if you want to make changes from the defaults, a UNIX command will allow you to.

Displaying Terminal Settings

When entered without arguments, the set terminal command, **stty**, displays the current settings for your terminal, as shown in this example:

```
$ stty
speed 2400 baud; -parity hupcl
line = 2; swtch = ^@;
brkint -inpck icrnl -ixany onlcr cr0 nl0 tab0 bs0 vt0 ff0
echo echoe -echok
$ _
```

The four lines displayed under the command line describe the current settings for your terminal. Let's take a look at the five items on the first two lines. (For explanations of the remaining items on the second two lines, see Table 14-2.)

speed 2400 baud	The speed (also known as data rate, baud rate, or transmission rate) is 2400 bits per second.
– parity	Parity detection (error checking) is turned off and character size is 8 bits.
hupcl	Hang up the telephone line on the last close.
line = 2	Set the line discipline to 2 (which could be VT100, ANSI, or something else).
swtch = ∧@	The key combination for switching to the shell layer manager is CTRL @.

You can change any of the current settings at any time.

Changing Terminal Settings

If the current settings for your terminal don't match those of the host computer, you can change them by using the **stty** command followed by arguments. For example, to change the data rate to 1200, enable parity detection, and change the switch character to CTRL Z, you could enter this command line:

```
$ stty 1200 parity char swtch ^z
$ _
```

The preceeding command line doesn't change the way your terminal works; it just informs the system. To make actual changes in your terminal to match the settings of your host, you have to do one of two things:

- If you have a terminal that was built before 1985, you will probably have to check the terminal manual and push DIP switches into the desired positions.
- If you have a newer terminal, you can probably run a set-up program and make selections on the screen from a menu.

To display the settings that you have just made with the **stty** command shown previously, enter the **stty** command again without arguments:

```
$ stty
speed 1200 baud; parity hupcl
line = 2; swtch = ^z;
brkint -inpck icrnl -ixany onlcr cr0 nl0 tab0 bs0 vt0 ff0
echo echoe -echok
$ _
```

As you can see from the simple examples shown above, a hyphen (or minus sign) in front of a feature means that the feature is turned off. If there is no hyphen, the feature is turned on. The features used in the example above are among the most common. However, the **stty** command also supports about five dozen others, which you can set in about the same way.

UNIX takes care of terminal set-up for you automatically if you use one of the following obsolete terminals: Teletype Model 33 or 37, DEC VT05, G.E. TermiNet 300, Texas Instruments 700, Tektronix 4014. Just enter the **stty** command, followed by the appropriate abbreviation:

tty33	Teletype Model 33	**tn300**	G.E. TermiNet 300
tty37	Teletype Model 37	**ti700**	T.I. 700
vt05	DEC VT05	**tek**	Tektronix 4014

For example, if you have a Tektronix 4014, just enter:

```
$ stty tek
$ _
```

The stty Command in Detail

The rest of this section contains detailed information about the internal operation of terminals. If this doesn't interest you, you may want to skip this and go on to the section about setting tabs. Without arguments, the **stty** command gives only a partial listing of terminal options. If you want to display **all** options for your terminal, you have to use the −**a** argument on the **stty** command line, as shown here:

```
$ stty -a
speed 2400 baud; line = 2; intr = DEL; quit = ^\;
erase = ^H; kill = ^U; eof = ^D; eol = ^@; swtch = ^@
-parenb -parodd cs8 -cstopb hupcl cread -clocal -loblk
 -ctsflow -rtsflow
-ignbrk brkint -ignpar -parmrk -inpck istrip -inlcr -igncr
 icrnl -iuclc
ixon -ixany -ixoff
isig icanon -xcase echo echoe -echok -echonl -noflsh
opost -olcuc onlcr -ocrnl -onocr -onlret -ofill -ofdel cr0
nl0 tab0 bs0 vt0 ff0
$ _
```

For a coded version of the display, you can use the −**g** argument to show the settings in **stty** argument format, as shown here:

```
$ stty -g
522:5:4bb:1b:7f:1c:8:15:4:0:0:0
$ _
```

The terminal operation modes used by the **stty** command are summarized in Table 14-2.

Table 14-2. Terminal Modes

Name	*Description*
cs*n*	Set character size to *n* bits (5, 6, 7, or 8)
line=*n*	Set line discipline to *n* (0–127)
char *c*	Set one of the following control characters (default value shown in parentheses):
	eof End of file (CTRL D or EOT)
	erase Erase the character left of the cursor (#)
	intr Interrrupt signal to terminal a process (Rubout or DEL)
	kill Erase the command line (@)
	quit Quit signal to create a core image file (CTRL L or FS)
	swtch Switch to shell control layer (CTRL Z or SUB)
rate	Set the data rate (110, 300, 600, 1200, 1800, 2400, 4800, 9600, 19200, or 38400)
sane	Reset to modes that work for most terminals (character size 7, enable and generate parity, even parity, enable modem control, and so on)

Table 14-2. Terminal Modes *(Cont'd)*

Name	Description
term	Set up one of the default terminals (tty33, tty37, vt05, tn300, ti700, or tek)
ek	Set erase to # and kill to @
0 (zero)	Hang up the telephone line immediately
raw	Enable raw input and output
−raw	Disable raw input and output
tabs	Preserve tabs
−tabs	Convert tabs to spaces
lcase	Allow lowercase letters (same as −LCASE)
−lcase	Allow uppercase letters (same as LCASE)
−LCASE	Allow uppercase letters (same as −lcase)
LCASE	Allow lowercase letters (same as lcase)
nl	Do not convert input carriage returns to newlines or output newlines to carriage returns
−nl	Convert input carriage returns to newlines and output newlines to carriage returns
parenb	Enable parity detection
−parenb	Disable parity detection
parodd	Set odd parity
−parodd	Set even parity
parity	Enable **parenb**; set **cs** to 7
−parity	Disable **parenb**; set **cs** to 8
evenp	Enable **parenb**; set **cs** to 7
−evenp	Disable **parenb**; set **cs** to 8
oddp	Enable **parenb**; set **cs** to 7
−oddp	Disable **parenb**; set **cs** to 8
cread	Enable receiver
−cread	Disable receiver
clocal	Disable modem control
−clocal	Enable modem control
cstopb	Use two stop bits
−cstopb	Use one stop bit
hupcl	Hang up on the last close
−hupcl	Do not hang up on the last close
hup	Hang up on last close
−hup	Do not hang up on last close
loblk	Block output from a layer that is not current
−loblk	Do not block output from a layer that is not current

Name	Description
	Modes that control terminal input:
brkint	Interrupt signal on break
−**brkint**	No interrupt signal on break
icrnl	Convert carriage returns to newlines
−**icrnl**	Do not convert carriage returns to newlines
ignbrk	Ignore break
−**ignbrk**	Do not ignore break
igncr	Ignore carriage returns
−**igncr**	Do not ignore carriage returns
ignpar	Ignore parity errors
−**ignpar**	Do not ignore parity errors
inlcr	Convert newlines to carriage returns
−**inlcr**	Do not convert newlines to carriage returns
inpck	Enable parity checking
−**inpck**	Do not enable parity checking
istrip	Strip characters to lowercase
−**istrip**	Do not strip characters to lowercase
iucic	Convert uppercase to lowercase
−**iucic**	Do not convert uppercase to lowercase
ixany	Use any character to restart output
−**ixany**	Use XON to restart output
ixoff	Enable XON/XOFF input control
−**ixoff**	Disable XON/XOFF input control
ixon	Enable XON/XOFF output control
−**ixon**	Disable XON/XOFF output control
parmrk	Mark parity errors
−**parmrk**	Do not mark parity errors
	Modes that control terminal output:
bs$n$	Set backspace delay to n (0 or 1)
cr$n$	Set carriage return delay to n (0-3)
ff$n$	Set form feed delay to n (0 or 1)
nl$n$	Set newline delay to n (0 or 1)
ocrnl	Convert carriage returns to newlines
−**ocrnl**	Do not convert carriage returns to newlines
ofdel	Set fill character to DEL
−**ofdel**	Set fill character to null
ofill	Use fill characters for delay
−**ofill**	Use timing characters for delay

Table 14-2. Terminal Modes *(Cont'd)*

Name	Description
olcuc	Convert lowercase to uppercase
−olcuc	Do not convert lowercase to uppercase
onlcr	Convert newlines to carriage returns
−onlcr	Do not convert newlines to carriage returns
onlret	Insert carriage return after newline
−onlret	Do not insert carriage return after newline
onocr	Do not output carriage returns at column zero
−onocr	Output carriage returns at column zero
opost	Post-process output
−opost	Do not post-process output
tab*n*	Set output delay after *n* horizontal tabs (0–3)
vt*n*	Set output delay after *n* vertical tabs (0 or 1)
	Modes that control local operation:
echo	Echo all input
−echo	Do not echo all input
echok	Echo newline after the kill character
−echok	Do not echo newline the kill character
echonl	Echo newlines
−echonl	Do not echo newlines
icanon	Enable erase and kill characters
−icanon	Disable erase and kill characters
isig	Enable checking for interrupt and quit signals
−isig	Disable checking for interrupt and quit signals
lfkc	Echo newline after the kill character
−lfkc	Do not echo newline the kill character
noflsh	Flush buffers after interrupt and quit signals
−noflsh	Do not flush buffers after interrupt and quit signals
stappl	Use application mode on a synchronous line
−stappl	Use line mode on a synchronous line
lstflush	Enable flush on a synchronous line
−lstflush	Disable flush on a synchronous line
−strap	Disable long line truncation on a synchronous line
−strap	Enable long line truncation on a synchronous line
xcase	Processed upper/lowercase presentation
−xcase	Unprocessed upper/lowercase presentation

If you request **raw** mode, the system accepts every keystroke literally; if you request **cooked** mode (the default), the system accepts only completed command lines. For example, suppose you type **datw** instead of **date** and then correct the mistake on the command line before pressing ENTER. These two lines show what the system accepts as input for each mode:

datw ^ he   Raw

date   Cooked (the default mode)

As you can see from Table 14-2, you have many terminal features to choose from. However, you probably won't need to use very many of them.

Setting Tabs

Unless you specify otherwise, the system places a tab stop every eight columns, starting in column 1. That is, the tabs are set for columns 1, 9, 17, 25, and so on. This should be adequate for most occasions. However, if you want to set the tabs another way, you can use the **tabs** command.

Entering the Tab Columns

One way you can use the **tabs** command is to specify where you want the tab stops set. For example, if you want them set every five columns (at 1, 6, 11, 16, and so on), you can enter the command line:

```
$ tabs -5
$ _
```

You can also enter a set of irregular tab stops:

```
$ tabs 1, 7, 15, 18, 26, 49
$ _
```

You can also use one of the command's built-in arguments to select tabs for a number of different programming languages. For a partial listing, see Table 14-3.

For example, to select tabs suitable for writing FORTRAN programs, you could enter the following command line:

```
$ tabs -f
$ _
```

Table 14-3. Tabs for Computer Languages

Argument	Programming Language	Tab Settings
−a	IBM S/370 assembler	1, 10, 16, 36, 72
−c	COBOL	1, 8, 12, 16, 20, 55
−f	FORTRAN	1, 5, 9, 13, 17, 21, 25, 29, 33, 37, 41, 45, 49, 53, 57, 61
−p	PL/I	1, 10, 55
−s	SNOBOL	1, 10, 55

The Terminal Information File

For programs like **vi** that use the entire screen, the system must have a description of your terminal. Before System V, coded descriptions of terminals were stored in a terminal capability file called **/etc/termcap**. Bill Joy and others developed **termcap** at the University of California in the 1970s. If your system has a **termcap** file, all terminal descriptions are stored in alphabetical order in this one file. The simplest descriptions are a line or two long; the most complex can be longer than 40 lines.

Beginning with System V, AT&T introduced a different scheme for describing terminals. In this scheme, a terminal information directory called **/usr/lib/terminfo** replaces the single **termcap** file. The **terminfo** directory includes 36 subdirectories, one for each letter of the alphabet and one for each digit. Then all the descriptions of terminals whose names begin with A are stored in the **a** subdirectory (**/usr/lib/terminfo/a**), those with names beginning with B are stored in the **b** subdirectory, and so on.

The individual terminal descriptions in **termcap** are similar to those in **terminfo**. However, a major difference is that the descriptions in **terminfo** are compiled before they are stored. This means that you can read **termcap** descriptions, but you can't read **terminfo** descriptions. With either scheme, each terminal entry contains four names for the terminal, followed by the codes that describe its functions. In **termcap**, these codes are separated by colons (:); in **terminfo,** they are separated by commas.

A termcap Example

As an example of a **termcap** entry, we'll use the Lear-Siegler ADM-3, which is very simple and easy to describe:

```
l∃|adm∃|∃|lsi adm∃:bs:am:li#24:co#80:cl=^Z
```

This one-line entry, probably the shortest in **termcap**, is in two parts: the names and the descriptions. Here are the four names:

```
l∃¦adm∃¦∃¦lsi adm∃
```

Here are the five descriptions, with comments in Table 14-4.

```
bs:am:li # 24:co # 80:cl=^Z
```

Table 14-4. Descriptions for termcap

Function	Comment
bs	Backspacing. The terminal can move the cursor back and erase the character to the left.
am	Automargins. The terminal can wrap text from the last column on the right side of the screen to the first column of the next line.
li#24	Lines. The terminal has 24 lines of display.
co#80	Columns. The terminal has 80 columns.
cl = ^Z	Clearing the screen. You can clear the terminal's screen by pressing CTRL Z.

A terminfo Example

The entry for the same ADM-3 terminal is compiled and stored in **/usr/lib/terminfo/a/adm3**. Before the entry is compiled, it looks like this, including four additional functions on the second line:

```
l∃^ad∃^∃^lsi adm∃,    cub1=^H, am, lines # 24, cols # 80. clear=^Z,
                      cud1=^J, ind=^J, cr=^M, bel=^G
```

The four names for the terminal are exactly the same for **terminfo**. The first five functions are the same, but the notation is different. In the example above, you see **cub1 = ^H** (with the backspacing combination CTRL H included) instead of **bs**, **lines** instead of **li**, **cols** instead of **co**, and **clear** instead of **cl**. The remaining functions, shown on the second line of the entry, are listed in Table 14-5.

Table 14-5. Descriptions for terminfo

Function	Comment
cud1 = ^J	Cursor down. Press CTRL J to move the cursor down one line.
ind = ^J	Index. Same as cursor down.
cr = ^M	Carriage return. Carriage return is CTRL M.
bel = ^G	Bell. Press CTRL G to sound the beeper.

Identifying Your Terminal

If **termcap** or **terminfo** includes an entry for your terminal, you can assign its name to the shell terminal variable **TERM**. You can do this on the command line, but it is much more convenient to do it in your initialization file. The assignment statements are shown here for the Bourne shell (**.profile**) and the C shell (**.login**):

Bourne shell	*C shell*
TERM = vt100	setenv TERM vt100
export TERM	

The **termcap** and **terminfo** databases contain many terminal entries. If your terminal isn't included, someone will have to write an entry for you and store it in the appropriate terminal description file. You can write the entry yourself, but you will have to study your terminal's programming manual and the **termcap** or **terminfo** description in the UNIX manual.

If you want to learn more about **termcap**, you may be interested in the following references:

Merritt, Douglas R., *The Termcap Reference Manual*, San Francisco: International Technical Seminars, Inc., 1985.

Strang, John, *Reading and Writing Termcap Entries*, Newton, Mass.: O'Reilly & Associates, 1987.

The **termcap** and **terminfo** files allow entries for printers as well as terminals. The syntax and notation are the same for printers and terminals. XENIX also has a file called **/etc/ttytype** that links terminal models described in **termcap** or **terminfo** with terminal ports listed in **/etc/ttys**. Each line entry in **/etc/ttytype** includes a terminal name from **termcap** or **terminfo**, followed by the name of a terminal port from **/etc/ttys**, as shown here:

```
$ cat /etc/ttytype
ansi tty01
ansi tty02
vt100 tty03
vt100 tty04
unknown tty05
unknown tty06
...
$ _
```

CHAPTER **15**

MANAGING PRINTERS

In DOS, you can control the operation of your printer by controlling the port to which it is connected. Printers are generally connected to personal computers through parallel ports, but PostScript printers are often connected through serial ports. However, serial ports are used mainly for outside communication. The ports supported by DOS are shown in Table 15-1.

Table 15-1. DOS Ports Supported

Name	Description	Name	Description
COM1	Serial port 1	LPT1	Parallel port 1
COM2	Serial port 2	LPT2	Parallel port 2
COM3	Serial port 3*	LPT3	Parallel port 3
COM4	Serial port 4*		

* Beginning with Version 3.3

If you have a dot-matrix printer, you can make two minor adjustments with the MODE command:

- The number of columns per line (80 or 132)
- The number of lines per inch (6 or 8).

For example, you can switch to 132 columns per line and 8 lines per inch by entering the following:

```
C:\> MODE LPT1: 132,8
LPT1: set for 132
Printer lines per inch set
C:\> _
```

As you can probably guess, the features for controlling the printers in a UNIX system are considerably more complex. Starting with System V, a UNIX system can have many printers—all under the control of a central queueing system. Furthermore, you can group like printers together into *classes*. When you have something to print, you can request printing either on a specific printer or on one of the printers in a class. In this chapter, you will learn how to set up the printer system and how to use the commands that control the printer system.

Setting Up Printers

In Chapter 5, "Utility Programs," you learned how to operate the **lp** printer system. Now you will learn how to prepare this system for operation.

Making a Connection

As noted at the beginning of this chapter, you can connect a printer through either a parallel port or a serial port. To connect a parallel printer to your system, all you have to do is plug in the cable. This is because all parallel cables are exactly the same. However, a serial printer can be more difficult to connect because serial cables vary widely.

Connecting a Serial Device

By far the most common type of serial connection on DOS systems as well as UNIX systems is RS-232C. This standard (or semistandard) for serial cables specifies voltage levels and provides some general guidelines about signal definitions. Out of 25 possible wires, frequently no more than three are actually used for a given connection. So RS-232C is anything but consistent, but here is an attempt to put all the pieces together.

RS-232C cables sometimes use 25-pin connectors, and sometimes use 9-pin connectors, depending on how many wires are required and how much space is available for the connector. The configuration of the 25-pin connector is shown in Figure 15-1.

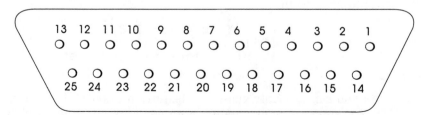

Figure 15-1. 25-Pin Cabling

A wire in an RS-232C cable attached to pin 2 at one end may be attached to pin 2 at the other end. However, the wire may connect pin 2 to another pin at the other end. It depends on how the devices being connected by the cable are defined. At first, RS-232C was used mainly to connect terminals to modems. The terminal was called the *data terminal equipment* (DTE) and the modem was called the *data communication equipment* (DCE). There was a match between the two because DTE transmits on pin 2 and receives on pin 3, while DCE receives on pin 2 and transmits on pin 3.

Over the years, printers and computers began to adopt the standard, but there was never any agreement about whether one of them was DTE or DCE. Some computers are designed as DTE and some as DCE, and it's the same with printers. If a particular computer is DTE and a particular printer is DCE, you may be able to connect the two with only three wires (see Table 15-2).

Table 15-2. DTE-to-DCE Connection

Computer (DTE)		Printer (DCE)	
Pin	Function	Pin	Function
2	Transmit data	2	Receive data
3	Receive data	3	Transmit data
7	Signal ground	7	Signal ground

Because the first wire connects pin 2 on the computer to pin 2 on the printer, pin 3 to pin 3, and pin 7 to pin 7, this is known as "straight-through" cabling. On pin 2, data always flows from the computer to the printer; on pin 3, it always flows from the printer to the computer.

The other possibility is that the computer and printer are both alike. For example, suppose the computer and printer are both DTE. Then you will have to cross the wires for pins 2 and 3, rather than connect them straight across, as shown in Table 15-3.

Table 15-3. DTE-to-DTE Connection

Computer (DTE)		Printer (DTE)	
Pin	Function	Pin	Function
2	Transmit data	2	Transmit data
3	Receive data	3	Receive data
7	Signal ground	7	Signal ground

As shown in Table 15-4, the two machines are both DTE, and you have to cross one wire from pin 2 on the computer to pin 3 on the printer and the other wire from pin 2 on the printer to pin 3 on the computer. This is sometimes called "cross-over" cabling.

For the examples in Tables 15-2 and 15-3, three wires were sufficient to form complete connections between the the two machines. However, many machines also require additional control signals to operate smoothly. The ten most common signals, including the three already discussed, are shown in Table 15-4.

Table 15-4. Common RS-232C Signals

No.	Short Name	Full Name	Direction DTE	DCE
1	FG	Frame Ground	N/A	N/A
2	TD/RD	Transmit/Receive Data	Out	In
3	RD/TD	Receive/Transmit Data	In	Out
4	RTS	Request to Send	Out	In
5	CTS	Clear to Send	In	Out
6	DSR	Data Set Ready	In	Out
7	SG	Signal Ground	N/A	N/A
8	DCD	Data Carrier Detect	In	Out
20	DTR	Data Terminal Ready	In	Out
22	RI	Ring Indicator	In	Out

When two machines are connected with RS-232C cables, they may use only three of the signals shown in Table 15-4 or they may use all ten signals. There is no consensus on how many signals are required for a particular connection. There is also no consensus on the function of any individual signal. Finally, there are no rules governing when signals should be held at fixed voltages and when they should be left to vary from one voltage level to another.

Once you've connected the machines, you have to be sure that the serial ports on both sides are set for the same transmission rate, the same word length, the same number of stop bits, and the same parity method. With a printer, you also have to make sure that you have it set to interpret tabs and newlines correctly. The **stty** command, described in the previous chapter, will handle most of these settings for you. Just take care to match the **stty** settings with the actual machine settings.

The Printing Queue

When you request printing on a UNIX system, your job is not routed directly to the printer. It is stored temporarily in the print spooling area (**/usr/spool/lp**) until the appropriate printer becomes available. Then a daemon called **lpsched** sends the file from the print spooling area to the printer, which is called **/dev/lp** or something similar.

Printing Example

Let's take another look at the printer classes that were described in Chapter 5, "Utility Programs," shown in Table 15-5.

Table 15-5. Three Printer Classes

wheel	matrix	laser
diablo	epson_1	lw
nec_1	epson_2	ljet_1
nec_2		ljet_2
qume		

According to Table 15-5, this system has nine printers grouped into three classes. There are four daisy-wheel printers, two dot-matrix printers, and three laser printers. We'll use these hypothetical printers and classes in some examples.

Administrative Printing Features

The **lp** printer system is a complete subsystem of UNIX. To work with this system, you have to log in as **lp** (line printer administrator), using home directory **/usr/spool/lp**. The commands are stored in **/usr/lib**, which should be included in your command execution path list.

The commands in this directory allow you to set up and configure the print spooling system, start and stop it, suspend and release individual printing jobs, and display detailed status information about the system. We'll begin with the commands for suspending printing.

Suspending Printing Jobs

If one of your printers needs temporary attention, you can suspend printing for a short time with the **disable** command. This will defer printing while you add paper, replace a ribbon, or remove a paper jam. Here is an example:

```
lp disable nec_2
printer "nec_2" now disabled
lp _
```

While you're taking care of the problem, all printing jobs for this printer will remain queued. Once the printer is ready to run again, you can resume operation by using this command:

```
lp enable nec_2
printer "nex_2" now enabled
lp _
```

On the other hand, if a printer is completely out of commission, you prevent jobs from being routed to it with the **reject** command. Suppose one of your printers has stopped working, and you have to call in a manufacturer's representative to repair it. You can turn off the machine and enter the following command:

```
lp reject nec_2
destination "nec_2" now rejecting requests
lp _
```

Now you can let someone work on the printer without disrupting the rest of the printing system. Once the printer has been repaired and ready to receive requests again, you can enter the following command to resume printing on this printer:

```
lp accept nec_2
destination "nec_2" now accepting requests
lp _
```

Turning the Spooler On and Off

You can use the **lpsched** command to turn the print spooling system on and **lpshut** to turn it off. You can enter each command from the shell prompt if you wish:

```
lp lpsched
lp _
```

But it's more convenient to place the command in the **rc** file. Then the print spooling system will be started automatically with the rest of the UNIX system. As long as the spooler is running and the spooler daemon is active, the system stores a lock file called **SCHEDLOCK** in directory **/usr/lib/lp**. This file prevents anyone from starting the spooler by mistake while it's running.

Configuring the Printing System

Before you can start the printing system, you have to identify each printer to the UNIX system and associate it with a logical device. The logical device is controlled by a printer interface program stored in **/usr/spool/lp/interface**. For the printer interface program, you can use either a program that comes with the UNIX system, known as a **model**, or a custom program that you write as a shell script.

To associate each printer with a printer interface program, use the command **/usr/lib/admin**. Before you can use **lpadmin**, you have to execute **lpshut** to turn off the printer system. Once the system is turned off, the **lpadmin** command associates a printer with a device and assigns a printer interface program. You can also use this command to perform other administrative tasks, as described below. Here is the general format of the **lpadmin** command:

```
                                      -mmodel
     lp lpadmin -pprinter -vdevice  [  -eprinter   ]
                                      -icustom
                                      other
```

where   **−p**_printer_ gives a printer name, consisting of 1–14 alphanumeric characters, including underscores.
−v_device_ gives the pathname of one of these: a hard-wired printer, a login terminal, or any other file to which **lp** can write.
−m_model_ gives the name of a model interface program stored in **/usr/spool/lp/model**.
−e_printer_ gives the name of an existing printer, whose interface program is to be used for the current printer.
−i_custom_ gives the name of a custom interface program stored in **/usr/lib/interface**.

other is one of the following additional options:
−h indicates a hard-wired printer.
−l indicates a login terminal.
−c_class_ adds a printer to _class_.
−r_class_ removes a printer from _class_.

When you assign a printer to a device, you have to identify a printer interface program on the same command line. You can identify the program by using one of the three arguments shown above (**−m**, **−e**, or **−i**). Each of the three is illustrated in the three examples that follow. In all the examples shown below, we assume that you have included **/usr/lib** in your command path list, allowing you to enter the **lpadmin** command without typing its full pathname.

Example 1. Choose a name from the list of interfaces furnished by **lp** in **/usr/spool/lp**. In this example, we'll use an interface called **epson**:

```
     lp lpadmin -pepson_1 -v/dev/tty31 -mepson
```

Example 2. Use the interface just defined to assign an interface program for another printer:

```
lp lpadmin -pepson_2 -v/dev/tty32 -eepson_1
```

Example 3. Use a custom program, called **prq**, that you have written your-self and stored in **/usr/spool/lp/interface**:

```
lp lpadmin -pqume -v/dev/tty33 -iprq
```

While you are assigning a printer to a device, you can do several other things at the same time: identify the printer's device as either a hard-wired printer or a login terminal; add the printer to a class or remove it from a class. Here are some examples:

Example 4. Identify the printer's device as a hard-wired printer with the −**h** argument:

```
lp lpadmin -pdiablo -v/dev/tty21 -h
```

Example 5. Identify the printer's device as a login terminal with the −**l** argument:

```
lp lpadmin -pqume -v/dev/tty22 -l
```

Example 6. Add printer **lw** to class **laser** with the −**c** argument:

```
lp lpadmin -plw -v/dev/tty51 -claser
```

Example 7. Remove printer **ljet_2** from class **laser** using the −**r** argument:

```
lp lpadmin -pljet_2 -v/dev/tty53 -rlaser
```

There are two more things you can do with the **lpadmin** when you aren't assigning a printer to a device: name the default printer or remove a printer from the printer spooling system. Two more examples follow.

Example 8. Designate printer **lw** as the default printer using the −**d** argu-ment:

```
lp lpadmin -dlw
```

Example 9. Remove printers **nec_1** and **nec_2** from the system using the −**x** argument:

```
lp lpadmin -xnec_1
lp lpadmin -xnec_2
lp _
```

Storage Locations

In the previous subsection, you learned how to use the **lpadmin** command. Now you will learn where information about the printer spooling system is stored in directory **/usr/spool/lp**. Table 15-6 gives the names of subdirectories of **/usr/spool/lp** with comments about their contents.

Table 15-6. Subdirectories of /usr/spool/lp

Name	Comments
member	Contains files with printer names; each file contains the name of its device. Referring to Example 1 above, file **/usr/spool/lp/epson_1** contains a one-line entry: /dev/tty31.
class	Contains files named after classes; each file contains the names of the printers that belong to the class. Referring to the spooling system shown in Table 15-4, file **/usr/spool/lp/class/matrix** contains two entries: /dev/tty31 /dev/tty32
model	Contains the names of default interface programs, which are also copied into **/usr/spool/lp/interface**.
request	Contains files named after printers; each file contains the text of all files queued to be printed on the printer named. For example, text to be printed on printer **ljet_1** is stored in **/usr/spool/lp/ljet_1**.
seqfile	Contains the sequence number of each printing request processed by the spooling system.
log	Contains a log entry (including sequence number, user's login name, device name, date, and time) for each printing request queued for processing.
oldfile	Contains log entries like those in **log** for printing requests already processed.
default	Contains the name of the default printer (if any).
output	Contains status information about printing requests.
outputq	Contains an output queue for the spooling system.

Checking Administrative Status

In Chapter 5, "Utility Programs," you learned how to use the **lpstat** command as an ordinary user to display the current printing queue. As a system administrator, you can use the − **t** argument with **lpstat** to display detailed information about the configuration of the spooling system as a whole. Here is an example:

```
# lpstat -t
scheduler is running
system default destination: lw
members of class wheel:
      diablo
      nec_1
      nec_2
      qume
device for diablo: /dev/tty21
device for nec_1: /dev/tty22
device for nec_2: /dev/tty23
device for qume: /dev/tty24
.
.

.
diablo accepting requests since Jan 4 10:34
nec_1 accepting requests since Jan 4 10:37
nec_2 accepting requests since Jan 4 10:46
qume accepting requests since Jan 5 09:12
.
.

.
#  _
```

The report displayed above indicates that the **lp** scheduler is running (that is, **lpsched** has been executed). It gives the name of the default printer (lw) and then proceeds to enumerate the names of the printers by class, followed by devices. After the enumeration of printer names, the report indicates the current status of each printer. Note that, for the sake of brevity, the report displayed above gives only information about printers in the first class (wheel).

Writing a Printer Interface Program

A printer interface program handles the actual printing for each printer active in the system. Directory **/usr/spool/lp/model** contains a set of model interface programs in the form of shell scripts. You can either use one of these or you can write your own program. Most are shell scripts, but you can also write your program in C, Pascal, or any other suitable language.

Whenever a user requests printing with an **lp** command line, the spooling system creates an information line and passes it to the printer interface program. The information line contains the fields that are described in Table 15-7.

The printer interface program uses the fields described in Table 15-7, as shown in this simple example. Line numbers, which aren't part of the script, have been added to make it easier to read the comments that follow.

Table 15-7. Fields for the Interface Program

Name	Description
$0	The name of the interface program, without **/usr/spool/lp**, such as **interface/prq**.
$1	The sequence number of the printing job, such as l – 3284.
$2	The login name of the requester, such as bill.
$3	An optional title, such as Monthly Sales. A user can request a title by using **lp −t** *title*.
$4	Number of copies to be printed, such as **5**. A user can request a number other than one by using **lp −n** n.
$5	Any other options entered on the **lp** command line, such as **− c** (copy), **− m** (mail), **− s** (suppress messages), or **− w** (write).
$6	Full pathname(s) of file(s) to printed, such as **/usr/bill/admin/sales.mar**.

```
    $ cat /usr/spool/lp/interface/prq
1.  #
2.  # Simple lp(1) interface
3.  #
4.  # Form feed:
5.  echo "\014\c"
6.  #
7.  # Banner the user's name:
8.  banner "$2"
9.  echo
10. echo "Request id: $1  Printer: "basename $0"\n"
11. date
12. echo "\n"
13. #
14. # Banner the title (if any):
15. title=$3
16. if [ -n "$title" ]
17. then
18.         banner $title
19. fi
20. echo "\014\c"
21. copies=$4
22. shift; shift; shift; shift; shift
23. files="$*"
24. i=1
25. while [ $1 -le $copies ]
26. do
27.         for file in $files
```

```
28.          do
29.                    cat "$file" 2 > &1
30.                    echo "\014\c"
31.          done
32.          i = "expr $1 +1"
33. done
34. exit 0
    $ _
```

In lines 4–12, the script generates a form feed and prints the user's login name, the sequence number, the name of the printer, and the date on a cover page. In lines 14–20, the script creates a banner title on the same page, with another form feed on line 20.

On line 21, the script picks up the number of copies to be printed, using variable **copies**. In line 22, the script shifts past the first five fields, making the sixth field, which is the name of the first file to be printed, the new first field. Then in line 23, it picks up the names of the files, using variable **files**.

The loop set up in lines 24 through 33 outputs the contents of each file, redirects any diagnostic messages to the screen, and generates a form feed. Finally, line 34 indicates successful completion of the printing request.

## CHAPTER 16

STARTUP AND SHUTDOWN

Introduction

Starting up a system and shutting it down are basic procedures in any operating system. Because UNIX is designed for more than one user, its procedures are considerably more complex than those for DOS.

Starting Up a DOS System

Starting up a DOS system is relatively easy. You just turn on the machine, enter the date and time, and go to work. If your system has a built-in clock, you don't even have to enter the date and time. There is still a lot going on inside the machine, even though you may not be directly involved in it. First of all, your machine probably runs self-diagnostics to check out all the major subsystems. Then your **AUTOEXEC.BAT** file takes over and does the rest.

In Chapter 9, "Batch Files and Initialization Files," we considered the following sample **AUTOEXEC.BAT** file. Let's look at it now in greater detail, with the aid of line numbers for reference.

```
    C:\> TYPE AUTOEXEC.BAT
 1. ECHO OFF
 2. CLS
 3. VER
 4. PROMPT=$P$G
 5. PATH C:\VENTURA;C:\WP50;C:\MISC
 6. DATE
 7. TIME
 8. CHKDSK C:
 9. DIR
    C:\> _
```

An explanation of each line is given in Table 16-1.

Table 16-1. Functions of Sample AUTOEXEC.BAT

Line	Action
1	You request that the commands that follow not be displayed on the screen, just executed.
2	Clear the screen.
3	Display the version number for DOS.
4	Set the prompt to display the current pathname ($P), followed by a greater than symbol ($G).
5	Whenever you enter a command, search the three directories named (in addition to the root directory): C:\VENTURA, C:\WP50, and C:\MISC. (Usually the list is longer.)
6	Prompt the user to enter today's date.
7	Prompt the user to enter the current time.
8	Run **CHKDSK** to check the integrity of your files on disk C.
9	Display the names of your files and main directories in root. (You should have only the most essential files here; all others should be moved to other directories.)

Many **AUTOEXEC.BAT** files are more complex than the one shown above. However, this one covers most bases and provides an adequate startingpoint for discussing start-up in a UNIX system.

Starting Up a UNIX System

Like DOS, UNIX also uses an initialization file to make it easier to start up the system. Actually, UNIX uses several files. To begin with, the main initialization file for the entire system, **/etc/rc** has been split up into three files, as of System V. In addition, once the system is up and running, each user has another initialization file. For a UNIX system with a dozen users, you have a total of 15 initialization files—three for the overall system and one for each user.

Then there's the issue of system shutdown. In DOS, all you have to do is exit from your application programs and turn off the machine. In UNIX, you can't just turn off the machine; you have to execute another shell script, called **/etc/shutdown**. Turning off the machine without running **shutdown** can cause a great deal of damage to your system.

This concludes the overview. Now we'll consider the steps to start up and shut down a UNIX system in detail.

UNIX Start-Up In Detail

Startup and shutdown procedures vary greatly from one UNIX installation to another. There is no possible way to cover all variations in an introductory chapter like this. All we can do is look at some of the most basic steps and hope that they are fairly representative. The actual procedures for your system may be quite different from those described in this chapter. But you should still learn from this chapter the main purpose for each step in starting up and shutting down a UNIX system.

Powering Up and Booting

The very first step is identical for both DOS and UNIX systems: turning on the power. In either case, you just flip the switch up to the ON position. The hum of motors should tell you when the power has started up. So far so good. Like a DOS system, a UNIX system will probably perform self-diagnostics.

Booting a system means copying its operating system from disk to memory and activating it. In DOS, booting takes place automatically after you turn on the power. In UNIX, it may or may not occur automatically; it varies from system to system.

In a system with many terminals, the primary terminal that is used for system administration is called the *console*. The console is usually the terminal closest to the host computer. However, starting with System V, you can designate any terminal in the system as the console. Since it isn't necessarily next to the host computer, it is referred to as the *virtual console*, or **/dev/syscon**.

On some systems, there may be additional prompts on the screen. If so, answer the prompts to complete the booting process. Once the system is booted, it starts out in *single-user mode* (or *maintenance mode*). At this point, *root* is the only file system known to UNIX. Always carry out system maintenance in single-user, or maintenance, mode.

Setting the Date and Time

Like DOS, UNIX requires a date and time for system record-keeping. However, UNIX doesn't prompt you for it; you have to enter it on your own with the **date** command. You enter both date and time on a single command line in a single argument in the format shown here, but without spaces:

```
month day hour minute [year]
```

Here is an example:

```
# date 0923081?
Mon Sep 23 08:17:01 PST 1990
# _
```

As long as the year hasn't changed since the last start-up, you can omit the year from the date and time string. A record of each clock-setting and each user login is maintained in a file called **/etc/wtmp.**

Checking File Systems

The file system check command, **fsck**, performs a thorough check on the integrity of your files. This program, which corresponds roughly to the DOS CHKDSK command, is probably more similar to the reconstruction tools in the Norton Utilities. In a UNIX system, **fsck** is absolutely essential. You must run this program in single-user mode every time you start up the system, which means you must place it in your **/etc/rc** file.

Without going into great technical detail, a UNIX file system is more fragile than its DOS counterpart. In DOS, each file is stored independently, according to information in the system's file allocation table (FAT); in UNIX, all files are closely interrelated in a hierarchy that begins with the root directory. An error in one file in a UNIX system can spread to other files successively, causing greater and greater damage to the file system. You need **fsck** for protection.

In general, a UNIX file system is an organized collection of *blocks* (where one block = 1,024 bytes). The system maintains two lists: one for blocks that contain data and one for blocks that do not. The list of unoccupied blocks is called the *free list*. Information about files, including their locations, is stored in records called index nodes, or *i-nodes*. The job of **fsck** is to perform what you might call a system audit. This audit watches the totals for the two lists and scans i-nodes to make sure there are no overlaps or gaps in individual files.

If you were to run **fsck** manually without encountering any errors, the display would look something like this:

```
# /etc/fsck
** Phase 1 - Check Blocks
** Phase 2 - Check Pathnames
** Phase 3 - Check Connectivity
** Phase 4 - Check Reference Counts
** Phase 5 - Check Free List
782 files  5846 blocks  2134 free
# _
```

If **fsck** encounters errors, it will ask you if you want to correct them. The safest strategy is to say no on the first run while you determine the extent of the damage. Then you can say yes to corrections on a subsequent run. For more detailed information about running **fsck** and making corrections, see *A System V Guide to UNIX and XENIX* by Douglas Topham, Springer-Verlag, New York, 1990, Chapter 29, "File Systems."

Logging In

Once you've determined that the system is free of errors, enter the following command to leave single-user mode and enter multiuser mode:

```
# init 2
```

You may or may not have to press CTRL D to proceed. In either event, the system will prompt you to log in:

```
login: root
Password:
# _
```

Naturally, if you log in as an ordinary user, you will see an ordinary shell prompt.

Initializing the UNIX System

When the system leaves single-user mode and enters multiuser mode, it is said to change states. Each time the system changes states, the shell usually runs initialization script **/etc/rc**, which corresponds roughly to **AUTOEXEC.BAT** in DOS. Here is a very simple example:

```
  # cat /etc/rc
1. PATH=/etc:/bin:/usr/bin
2. cat dev/null > /etc/utmp
3. /etc/fsck
4. /etc/mount /dev/dsk/c0d1s3 /usr
5. rm -f /tmp/*
6. rm -f /usr/tmp/*
7. /etc/update
8. /etc/cron
  # _
```

Each line is described in Table 16-2.

Table 16-2. Functions of Sample /etc/rc

Line	Action
1	Set up your command path list: **/etc/**, **/bin**, and **/usr/bin**.
2	Empty the list of logged-in users from the previous startup.
3	Start **fsck** to check the file system.
4	Mount user directory **/usr**.
5	Remove temporary files.
6	Remove more temporary files.
7	Start **update** to keep files up to date.
8	Start **cron** (timed processes).

The purpose of the simple example shown above is to compare **/etc/rc** with **AUTOEXEC.BAT**. But in System V, **/etc/rc** has actually been divided into three different files, as shown in Table 16-3.

Table 16-3. Initialization Files

File	Purpose
/etc/brc	Restore the mount table **/etc/mnttab**.
/etc/bcheckrc	Set the date and time; check the file systems with **fsck**.
/etc/rc	Mount the file systems; start accounting processes and daemons (if any); back up the logs for **cron** and the superuser; remove temporary files; start the print-spooling system.

Operating In Multiuser Mode

In multiuser mode, all devices and file systems are active and functioning. Now we'll consider what takes place in a UNIX system when a user logs in. It's more involved than you might expect.

Logging in as a User

While the system is changing to multiuser mode, a process called **init** reads a file named **/etc/inittab** to find out which terminal lines are active. To each active line **init** assigns a process called **getty**, and the sequence has begun.

Each **getty** process reads a file named **/etc/gettydefs** to learn about the terminal. Then **getty** displays a login prompt on the terminal's screen and waits for something to happen. As soon as a user enters a login name, **getty** hands over the login name to another process called login.

The login process searches for the name in **/etc/passwd**. If it finds the name, it reads the user's password, displays a password prompt, and waits for a response. If the user (or non-user) enters an incorrect password, login informs the user (or non-user) and invokes **getty** again, and the sequence starts all over. If the user (or non-user) enters the correct password, login looks at **/etc/passwd** again to find the user's group, home directory, and login program. Then the login program, usually one of the shells, takes over.

If it's the Bourne shell, it starts by running a program called **/etc/profile** to perform any initialization tasks that may be set up for all terminals. Usually /**etc/profile** reads a file called **/etc/motd** to display the message of the day. If the shell finds an initialization file (**.profile**) in the user's home directory, it executes it and displays the shell prompt on the screen. The default prompt is a dollar sign ($).

If the login program is the C shell, it starts by executing a shell script in the user's home directory called **.cshrc**. From the **.cshrc** script, the shell obtains any secondary prompt, a history setting, and any aliases the user may have set up. Then the shell executes the user's **.login** script, which provides the primary shell prompt, terminal settings, a command search path, and possibly a message to the user. The default prompt is a percent sign (%).

The login sequence is summarized in Table 16-4.

Table 16-4. The Login Sequence

Step	Screen Prompt	Process	Files Referred to
1.		init	/etc/inittab
2.	login:	getty	/etc/gettydefs
3.	Password:	login	/etc/passwd
4.	$	sh	/etc/profile, $HOME/.profile
	%	csh	$HOME/.cshrc, $HOME/.login

In step 4, the login program takes over. The login program is usually one of the command processors, the Bourne shell or the C shell.

The Initialization Command

Now we'll take a closer look at the **init** command, which sets up the modes, or levels, at which the UNIX system can run. You've already learned about the transition from single-user to multiuser mode. The **init** command works through the initialization table, **/etc/inittab**, which contains a list of all the processes that the system activates upon transition to a given level. Here is an example of a line in the initialization table:

```
07:2:respawn:/etc/getty tty07
```

This entry contains four fields, separated from each other by colons (:). Here are the four fields separated and labeled with headings:

Name	Level	Action	Command
07	2	respawn	/etc/getty tty07

The four fields in this entry have a message for **init**: "Whenever the system enters level 2, find out if a **getty** for terminal 07 is running. If it isn't running, respawn it." Whenever you execute **init 2** to change to multiuser mode (level 2), **init** activates the entry shown above.

A real initialization table contains many lines like the preceding one. Here is an example of an abbreviated table:

```
$ cat /etc/inittab
is:s:initdefault:
bt:2:bootwait:rm -f /etc/mnttab > /dev/console
bl:2:bootwait:/etc/bcheckrc > /dev/console 2>&1
wt:2:bootwait:/etc/wrmpclean > /dev/console
bc:2:bootwait:/etc/brc > /dev/console
rc:2:wait:/etc/rc 1>/dev/console 2>&1
pf::powerful:/etc/powerfail 1>/dev/console 2>&1
ka:s:sysinit:killall
co:23:respawn:/etc/getty console console
00:23:respawn:/etc/getty tty00 4800
01:23:respawn:/etc/getty tty01 2400
02:23:respawn:/etc/getty tty02 1200
03:23:respawn:/etc/getty tty03 1200
04:23:off:/etc/getty tty04 9600
$ _
```

The four fields are described fully in Table 16-5.

If it becomes necessary to activate an inactive terminal in multiuser mode (or deactivate an active terminal), the procedure is very simple. To activate a terminal, use **vi** to edit the **/etc/inittab**, move to the desired line, and change **off** to **respawn** in the action field. To deactivate a terminal, change **respawn** to **off**. Then enter this command line to put the change into effect:

```
# init q
# _
```

Executing **init q** starts all processes in **/etc/inittab** that have been modified without changing the run level. If the **getty** process for a terminal that you are deactivating is still running, you may have to stop it by using the **kill** command.

Table 16-5. Fields in /etc/inittab

Field	Description
Name	One or two characters to identify the line.
Level	The run level (or levels) at which the action named is to be carried out. You can use one or more of the following: s or 0–6. Some of these are predefined: s Single-user mode 2 Multiuser mode 3 Remote File Sharing (RFS) mode An empty field means all levels. You can type numbers consecutively (such as 23) or give a range (such as 2–4).
Action	One of the words listed below to indicate what to do at the run level given on this line:
	initdefault Default level after booting
	sysinit Run the command named before before interacting with the system console
	bootwait Run the command after booting and wait for the process to complete
	wait Wait for the process to complete
	powerfail Run after a power failure
	respawn Start the process and restart it every time it completes
	off Terminate the process if it is currently running
Command	A command line to be executed, depending on what is specified by the action

UNIX Shutdown In Detail

A shell script called **/etc/shutdown** allows you to shut the system down correctly. This script will carry out these tasks in sequence:

1. Check the login name of the user who started **/etc/shutdown** to make sure that it's the system administrator.
2. Find out if any other users are still logged in. If they are, use the write-all command, **wall**, to notify them of the impending shutdown.
3. Halt process accounting, error-logging, all daemons, and the print-spooling system.
4. Execute the **sync** command to complete all remaining disk activity.
5. Run the **umount** command to unmount all mounted devices.
6. Execute **init s** to return to single-user mode.

UNIX COMMANDS

Command	Definition	Chapter

bc Start high-precision calculator **5**

$ bc [*options*] [*files*]

Option *Function*
-l Invoke the math library

cal Display a calendar **5**

$ cal [*month*] *year*
where
  month is a number from 1 to 12
  year is a number from 1 to 9999

calendar Send yourself a reminder **8**

$ calendar [-] [*year*]

Option *Function*
- Run **calendar** for all users who have calendar files

cat Display or concatenate files **3,5**

$ cat [*options*] *files*

Option *Function*
-s Suppress messages about non-existent files
-u Unbuffer output (Release 3)
-v Display non-printing characters (Release 3)
-t With −v only, display tab as ^I (Release 3)
-e With −v only, end each line with $ (Release 3)

cd Change directories **3**

$ cd [*directory*]

chmod Change file access permissions **3,12**

Command	Definition	Chapter

$ chmod *access files*

Symbol	Function
a	All (user, group, and others) (the default)
u	The user (or owner)
g	The user's working group
o	Other users (outside the user's group)
+	Add permission
−	Remove permission
=	Assign permissions absolutely
r	Permission to read
w	Permission to write
x	Permission to execute

cp   Copy file(s)   **3**

$ cp *file_1 file_2*
                or
$ cp *files directory*

cpio   Copy files   **13**

$ cpio -o [aBcv]   Copy out
$ cpio -i [Bcdfmrtuv] [*text*]   Copy in
$ cpio -p [adlmruv] *directory*   Pass

Option	Function
a	Update access times of input files
B	Copy blocks of 5,120 bytes per record
c	Include ASCII header information
d	Create needed directories
f	Copy all files except those named in *text*
l	Link instead of copy whenever possible
m	Retain modification times
r	Rename files through prompts
t	Table of contents: show names only
u	Unconditional: Copy the files
v	Verbose: Display filenames

cu   Call up another system   **8**

$ cu [*options*] *system*

Option	Function
−d	Show diagnostic messages
−e	Set even parity
−l*line*	Select a line name
−m	Use modem control
−n	Number: prompt for phone number
−o	Set odd parity
−s*rate*	Set the data rate

Command	Definition	Chapter
-t	Call an ASCII terminal	
system	Use a telephone number or a **uucp** name	

Commands used in **cu** sessions

Command	*Function*
~!	Escape from **cu** to the local shell
~!*command*	Run *command* on the local system
~$*command*	Run *command* on the local system and send output to the other system
~%cd	Change directories on local system (Release 2)
~%put *file*	Copy *file* to the other system
~%take *file*	Copy *file* from the other system
~.	Disconnect the two systems

| **dc** | Start desk calculator | 5 |

$ **dc** [*file*]

| **find** | Find files | 5 |

$ **find** *directories options*

Option	*Function*
-atime *d*	Match files accessed *d* days ago
-cpio *dev*	Write file to device *dev* in **cpio** format
-ctime *d*	Match files changed *d* days ago
-depth	List files and directories
-exec *cmd*	Execute command *cmd*
-group *name*	Match files in group *name*
-links *n*	Match files with *n* links
-mtime *d*	Match files modified *d* days ago
-name *name*	Match files named *name*
-newer *name*	Match files newer than file *name*
-ok *cmd*	Execute command *cmd* with confirmation
-print	Display filenames matched
-size *b*	Match files that are *b* blocks long
-type *x*	Match files (x = p) or directories (x = d)
-user *name*	Match files owned by user *name*

| **grep** | Find text in file(s) | 5 |

$ **grep** [*options*] *text* [*files*]

Option	*Function*
-c	Count matching lines
-i	Ignore case
-l	Display filenames only
-n	Display line numbers
-v	Display non-matching lines

| **ln** | Link a file | 3 |

Command	*Definition*	*Chapter*

$ ln *file_1 file_2*
            or
$ ln *files directory*

lp   Print file(s)   **5**

$ lp [*options*] *files*

Option	*Function*
-c	Make a copy of the file(s) before printing
-d*printer*	Direct printing to printer
-m	Mail message to user
-n*copies*	Print copies
-t*message*	Print banner
-w	Write a message to the user

lpstat   Display printing status   **5,15**

$ lpstat [*options*]

Option	*Function*
-c[*class*]	Display printers and classes
-d	Display name of default printer
-o[*items*]	Display status of printing requests (*items*=classes, printers, or printing requests)
-p[*prtrs*]	Display status of printers
-r	Display status of request scheduler
-s	Display a summary (same as **-cdru**)
-t	Display all status information
-u[*users*]	Display status of print requests
-v[*prtrs*]	Display printers with pathnames

ls   List names of files in a directory   **3,13**

$ ls [*options*] [*file*]

Option	*Function*
-a	Display all filenames
-C	Use multiple columns sorted from top to bottom
-F	Display / after directory name and * after name of executable file
-l	Long list in seven columns
-n	Long list with numeric user and group
-p	Display / after directory name
-r	Reverse order
-t	List by time of last modification
-u	List by time of last access
-x	Use multiple columns sorted from left to right

mail   Send or receive electronic mail   **8**

$ mail [*options*] [*users*]

Command	Definition	Chapter

Release 2

Option	Function
-e	Don't show messages
-f *file*	Use *file* instead of default mail file
-p	Display incoming mail without prompts
-r	Display mail in reverse order
-t	Names of all recipients before message

Code	Action
* (or ?)	List all commands
p	Redisplay message (print)
d	Delete message
m *user*	Forward message to *user*
s	Save message (with header) in file **mbox**
s *file*	Save message (with header) in *file*
w	Save message (without header) in file **mbox**
w *file*	Save message (without header) in *file*
Return	Display next message
! *command*	Escape to run *command*
q	Quit **mail** (leave only unread messages)
x	Exit **mail** (leave all messages)

Release 3

Option	Send Function
-o	Don't optimize addresses
-s	Don't begin with a newline
-t	Add "To" line
-w	For remote mail, don't wait for completion

Option	Receive Function
-e	Don't show mail
-F *user*	Forward mail to user(s)
-h	Show numbered list of messages
-f *file*	Use *file* instead of default mail file
-p	Show all incoming mail without prompts
-r	Show mail in reverse order

Code	Action
?	List all commands
n	Display message *n*
p	Print: Redisplay message
d	Delete message
dq	Delete message and quit
d *n*	Delete message *n*
m *user*	Forward message to *user*
s	Save message (with header) in file **mbox**
s *file*	Save message (with header) in *file*
w	Save message (without header) in file **mbox**
w *file*	Save message (without header) in *file*

Command	Definition	Chapter
–	Display previous message	
+	Display next message	
Return	Display next message	
h	Display some headers	
h a	Display all headers	
h d	Display headers for messages to be deleted	
h *n*	Display header for message *n*	
! *command*	Escape to run *command*	
q	Quit **mail** (leave only unread messages)	
x	Exit **mail** (leave all messages)	

mailx   Send or receive electronic mail   8

$ mailx [*options*] [*users*]

Option	Function
-e	Check for mail without reading
-H	Display headers without messages
-N	Display messages without headers
-s *header*	Set subject header
-U	Convert from **uucp** to **mailx**

Escape Command	Action
~?	List all escape commands
~s *subject*	Enter a subject title
~t *user(s)*	Add users to the "To" list
~c *user(s)*	Add users to the "Copy" list
~h	Prompt for "To," "Subject," and "Copy"
~r *file*	Read from another file
~w *file*	Write message to another file
~v	Edit message with **vi**
~p	Print: Display message
~f *message(s)*	Read other messages
~m *message(s)*	Read other messages (indented to tab stop)
~! *command*	Escape to run a UNIX command
~¦ *command*	Pipe message through UNIX command
~q	Quit (save message in file **dead.letter**)
~x	Exit (discard message)

?	List all commands with comments
list	List all commands without comments
header	Display active headers
z	Display next page of headers
z –	Display last page of headers
from [*list*]	Display header(s)
top [*list*]	Display first five lines of message(s)
next	Display next message
type [*list*]	Display message(s)
preserve [*list*]	Preserve message(s) in **mbox**
save [*list*] *file*	Append message(s) to *file*
delete [*list*]	Delete message(s)

Command	Definition	Chapter
undelete [*list*]	Undelete message(s)	
edit [*list*]	Edit message(s)	
Reply [*list*]	Reply only to sender(s)	
reply [*list*]	Reply to sender(s) and other recipients	
cd [*directory*]	Change to *directory* (home if name omitted)	
! *command*	Escape to run UNIX command	
quit	Quit (save only unread messages in **mbox**)	
xit	Exit (save all messages in **mbox**)	

mesg   Allow other users to write to your screen   **8**

    $ **mesg y**   Allow incoming messages
    $ **mesg n**   Prevent incoming messages

mkdir   Create a directory   **3**

    $ **mkdir** *directory*

mm   Format text to be printed   **7**

    $ **mm** [*options*] *file(s)*

Request	Function
.P 0	Block paragraph
.P 1	Ordinary paragraph
.DS *option*	Static display
.DF *option*	Floating display
I	Indented
I F *n*	Double-indented
C	Centered
CB	Blocked
.BL	Bullet list
.DL	Dash list
.ML *mark*	Mark list
.RL	Reference list
.VL	Variable-item list
.AL	Auto-numbered list
.SA 1	Justify text
.SA 0	Unjustify text
.SP *n*	Skip *n* lines
.I	Start italic
.B	Start bold
.R	Start roman
.S *p v*	Change point size and line spacing

mv   Rename or move file(s)   **3**

    $ **mv** *file_1 file_2*
           or
    $ **mv** *files directory*

nroff   Format text for fixed-wdth printer   **7**

Command	Definition	Chapter
`troff`	Format text for variable-width printer	

```
$ nroff [options] [files]
        or
$ troff [options] [files]
```

Option	Function
`-cx`	Process with macro package **m**x
`-e`	Space words equally in justified text
`-opages`	Print only *pages* as listed here
`-Tprinter`	Specify a particular printer
`p1-p2`	Print from page *p1* to page *p2*
`-p`	Print from beginning of file to page **p**
`p-`	Print from page *p* to the end of the file

Request	Function
`.pl n`	Page length *n* lines
`.po n`	Page offset *n* characters
`.pn n`	Page number *n*
`.bp`	Page break
`.ll n`	Line length *n* characters
`.in n`	Indent *n* characters
`.ti n`	Temporarily indent *n* characters
`.ne n`	Need vertical space (n lines)
`.fi`	Turn on filling
`.nf`	Turn off filling
`.ad`	Adjust text
`.na`	Do not adjust text
`.hy n`	Hyphenate after *n* characters
`.nh`	No hyphenation
`.br`	Break to a new page
`.ls n`	Line spacing *n*
`.ce`	Center a line
`.ce n`	Center the next *n* lines
`.ul`	Underline text
`.cu`	Continuously underline text
`%`	Place page number
`\u`	Superscript
`\d`	Subscript
`.TS`	Start of table
`.TE`	End of table
`.EQ`	Start of equation
`.EN`	End of equation

`nroff only`

`.1C`	Single column
`.2C`	Double column

`troff only`

Command	Definition	Chapter

.ps *n*   Change point size
\f*n*   Change point size (within a line)
.vs *n*   Change the vertical spacing to *n*
.ss *n*   Change the word spacing to *n*
.cs *fn*   Change to constant character spacing
.ft *n*   Select font number *n*
\f*n*   Select font number *n*
.fp *n f*   Change font positions

passwd   Change password   **2**

pg   Display large files   **5**

$ pg [*options*] [*files*]

Option	Function
-c	Home cursor and clear screen
-e	Do not pause at end of file
-f	Do not split wide lines
-n	Allow one-letter commands without **Enter**
-s	Highlight prompts and messages
+*line*	Start at line number
+/*string*/	Start at first occurrence of *string*

ps   Check process status   **4**

$ ps [*options*]

Option	Function
-a	Show all processes except process group leaders and those not started from terminals
-d	Show all processes except process group leaders
-e	Show all processes, not just your own
-f	Full list
-l	Long list

pwd   Display name of current directory   **3**

readnews   Look at the USENET bulletin board   **8**

$ readnews [*options*] [*newgroups*]

Option	Action
?	Help
N	Next newsgroup
U	Unsubscribe from current newsgroup
b	Back to previous article in current newsgroup
–	Back to previous article
+	Skip article
e	Erase memory of having read current article
s *file*	Save article in *file*
r	Reply to article

Command	Definition	Chapter
f	Follow-up article	
Del	Delete rest of article	
x	Exit	
rm	Delete file(s)	3

$ rm [*options*] *files*

Option	Function
-f	Remove files forcibly
-i	Remove files interactively
-r	remove all subdirectories and files, then directory

rmdir	Remove directory	3

$ rmdir *directory*

Option	Function
-p	Remove directories and empty parent directories (Release 3) and show directories removed
-r	Delete files from directories recursively
-s	Used with −p, omit directory names

sh	Shell	10

Shell Variables

HOME	Login directory
MAIL	Mail file
PATH	Command search path
TERM	Terminal type

PS1	Primary prompt
PS2	Secondary prompt
IFS	Internal file separator
TZ	Time zone
LOGNAME	Login name

Command	Function
<	Redirect command input
>	Redirect command output
>>	Redirect output and append
&	Run background process
echo *text*	Display text on screen
read *var*	Assign input to variable *var*
ps	Display status of background processes
nice *n*	Change priority of a process
kill *pppp*	Terminate background process *pppp*
shl	Start shell layer manager
p1 ¦ *p2*	Pipe *p1* to *p2*
p ¦ tee *file*	Tee: Display the output of *p* and redirect to *file*

Command	Definition	Chapter

Matching Patterns

?	Match any character
*	Match any characters
[*characters*]	Match any character enclosed

Positional Parameters

$0	Command
$1	First argument
$2	Second argument
$3	Third argument
...	
$*n*	The *n*th argument

sort Sort lines in file(s); merge sorted files **5**

$ **sort** [*options*] [*files*]

Option	*Function*
-b	Ignore spaces and tabs
-c	Make sure file is sorted
-d	Sort in dictionary order
-f	Fold uppercase into lowercase
-m	Merge sorted files
-M	Sort months
-n	Sort in numeric order
-o *file*	Sort to *file*
-r	Sort in reverse order
-u	Unique option: for identical lines, use only one
+*n*	Start sorting after *n* fields
-*m*	Stop sorting after *m* fields

su Change login name (root if no name) **12**

tee Redirect output and send to standard output **4**

$ **tee** [*options*] [*files*]

Option	*Function*
-a	Append to file
-i	Ignore **DEL** to interrupt processing

troff Format for variable-width printer **7**

See **nroff**

uucp UNIX-to-UNIX copy **8**

$ **uucp** [*options*] *files destination*

Option	*Function*
-C	Make a copy before queueing
-d	Create any required directories

Command		Definition	Chapter
	−f	Do not create directories	
	−m *file*	Mail message to *file* (default **mbox**) after completion	
	−n *user*	Notify recipient that a file is being sent	
uux		UNIX-to-UNIX execute	**8**

$ **uux** [*options*] *command*

Option	*Function*
−	Read from the standard input
−m *file*	Display status of *file*

vi	Edit text with full screen	**6**

$ **vi** [*options*] [*files*]

Option	*Function*
−r *file*	Recover *file* after system failure
−R	Read only
−t *tag*	Start at *tag* in the file that contains *tag*
−x	Edit encrypted file
+	Begin at end of file

Command	*Function*
h	Move cursor left one space
j	Move cursor down one line
k	Move cursor up one line
l	Move cursor right one space
b	Move to beginning of previous word
B	Move to beginning of previous word (ignore punctuation)
w	Move to beginning of next word
W	Move to beginning of next word (ignore punctuation)
e	Move to end of next word
E	Move to end of next word (ignore punctuation)
(	Move to beginning of sentence
)	Move to end of sentence
{	Move to beginning of paragraph
}	Move to end of paragraph
[	Move to beginning of section
]	Move to end of section
^	Move to beginning of line
$	Move to end of line
H	Move to top of screen
M	Move to middle of screen
L	Move to bottom of screen
CTRL U	Scroll up
CTRL D	Scroll down
CTRL B	Page back

Command	*Definition*	*Chapter*
CTRL F	Page forward	
a	Append text after cursor	
A	Append text at end of line	
I	Insert text at beginning of line	
i	Insert text before cursor	
O	Open new line above	
o	Open new line below	
cw	Change text to end of word	
cW	Change text to end of word (ignore punctuation)	
c^	Change to beginning of line	
c$	Change to end of line	
cc	Change entire line	
c(	Change to beginning of sentence	
c)	Change to end of sentence	
c{	Change to beginning of paragraph	
c}	Change to end of paragraph	
<<	Shift entire line left	
<(	Shift to beginning of sentence left	
<)	Shift to end of sentence left	
<{	Shift to beginning of paragraph left	
<}	Shift to end of paragraph left	
>>	Shift entire line right	
>(	Shift to beginning of sentence right	
>)	Shift to end of sentence right	
>{	Shift to beginning of paragraph right	
>}	Shift to end of paragraph right	
dw	Delete text to end of word	
dW	Delete text to end of word (ignore punctuation)	
d^	Delete to beginning of line	
d$	Delete to end of line	
dd	Delete entire line	
d(	Delete to beginning of sentence	
d)	Delete to end of sentence	
d{	Delete to beginning of paragraph	
d}	Delete to end of paragraph	
:w	Write text to disk file	
:w *name*	Write text to file *name*	
:wq	Write text to file and quit	
:q	Quit the editor	
:q!	Quit the editor and abandon text	
who	Show who is logged in	3,12

Option	*Function*
-a	Turn on all options except **-q** and **-s**

Command	*Definition*	*Chapter*
-b	Display date and time of last reboot	
-d	List all dead processes	
-H	Display headings above information	
-l	Display only idle lines (no login)	
-q	Quick **who**: Display only names and total (Release 2)	
-s	Display only name, line, and time	
-T	Include state (whether others can write to a given terminal)	
-u	Display only users currently logged in.	

write   Send message to terminal   **8**

$ write *user* [*terminal*]

Index

Characters and Symbols

& (ampersand)
    for background processes, 46
    used in redirection, 148

' (apostrophe; single quotation mark), for
    multiword shell variables, 149-150

* (asterisk)
    as wildcard character, 30
        in C shell, to reexecute commands, 169
        in timed execution of commands, 184
        used with **find** command, 63

@ (at sign), to erase command line, 16

\ (backslash)
    in **grep** command, 63-64
    in pathnames (DOS), 22
    for root directory (DOS), 21

{, } (braces)
    in command arguments, 59
    to move cursor, in **vi** (UNIX text editor), 80

[,] (brackets)
    in **grep** command, 63
    to test conditional statements, 155

^ (caret)
    in C shell, to reexecute commands, 168
    to move to beginning of line, 78

: (colon)
    in C shell, to reexecute commands, 168
    in **ex** (text editor) commands, 75-76
    for hardware devices, 21
    in **termcap** descriptions of terminals, 214

, (comma) in **terminfo**
    descriptions of terminals, 214

$ (dollar sign)
    to assign shell variables, 149
    in C shell, to reexecute commands, 169
    to move to end of line, 78
    for UNIX positional parameters, 138-139
    as UNIX shell prompt, 13, 38, 39, 235
    in use of shell variables, 150

= (equal sign) for assigning permissions, 33, 35

! (exclamation mark), in C shell, 129
    to reexecute commands, 166-167

' (grave accent mark), used in shell variables,
    152

> (greater-than symbol), for redirection, 42, 43,
    147, 148

- (hyphen)
    in dash lists, 106
    in **stty** command, for terminal set-ups, 208

<(less-than symbol), for redirection, 42, 147

- (minus sign)
    in command arguments, 15, 40
    for removing permissions, 33
    in **stty** command, for terminal set-ups, 208

(,) (parentheses)
    in C shell command search path, 164
    to move cursor, in **vi** (UNIX text editor),
    79-80

% (percent sign)
    for DOS positional parameters, 138
    as UNIX shell prompt, 13, 38, 39, 235

D

I

J

K

Q

R

V

W

X

ABOUT THE AUTHOR

Douglas Topham grew up in Los Angeles, then attended Stanford University. After teaching at the secondary and college levels, he worked briefly as a computer programmer. On one job he produced the screen displays for a game show on ABC television. He has also written *The WordStar Training Guide, UNIX and XENIX: A Step by Step Guide,* and *Introduction to WordPerfect.*